MATERIALITY AS RESISTANCE

Also by Walter Brueggemann
from Westminster John Knox Press

MATERIALITY
AS RESISTANCE

*Five Elements for Moral Action
in the Real World*

WALTER BRUEGGEMANN

Foreword by Jim Wallis

WJK WESTMINSTER
JOHN KNOX PRESS
LOUISVILLE · KENTUCKY

© 2020 Walter Brueggemann
Foreword and study guide © 2020 Westminster John Knox Press

First edition
Published by Westminster John Knox Press
Louisville, Kentucky

20 21 22 23 24 25 26 27 28 29—10 9 8 7 6 5 4 3 2 1

Scripture quotations from the New Revised Standard Version of the Bible are copyright © 1989 by the Division of Christian Education of the National Council of the Churches of Christ in the U.S.A. and are used by permission.

Book design by Erika Lundbom-Krift
Cover design by Mark Abrams
Cover image © Texture Fabrik

Library of Congress Cataloging-in-Publication Data is on file at the Library of Congress, Washington, D.C.

ISBN-13: 978-0-664-26626-4

Most Westminster John Knox Press books are available at special quantity discounts when purchased in bulk by corporations, organizations, and special-interest groups. For more information, please e-mail SpecialSales @wjkbooks.com.

CONTENTS

FOREWORD

A Compelling Worldly Faith

I LOVED READING THIS BOOK, WHICH REMINDS ME AGAIN that nobody does it better than Walter Brueggemann in applying the Bible to how to change the world. Indeed, that's what most of the Bible is about: how God is acting in the world and how God's people should act with their Creator. Walter has been the prophet to all the prophets of our age. His "prophetic imagination" has always to do with how we can partner with God's purposes in the world.

I could never understand how my church missed all this as I was growing up. Their favorite verse, and the one they forced me to memorize first (an experience that I know many people raised in evangelical churches will easily relate to) was, of course, John 3:16, "For God so loved the world, that he gave his only begotten Son, that whosoever believeth in him should not perish, but have everlasting life." (I used KJV 'cause that's what I memorized!) I memorized it, as have countless millions of others. And that solved it: the Christian life. Just believe this and you will go to heaven, and therefore not to hell (the worst fear that was drummed into us).

The problem is, my church completely ignored the very first part of the text: "For God so loved the world. . . ."

And "the world" had nothing to do with our faith, except that we were not to be "worldly." In fact, the world never came up in our church or its teaching, which instead focused on how to escape the world by believing in Jesus—never *following Jesus*, mind you, but just *believing* in him so you could have eternal life in heaven.

That became a problem for me as a teenager in Detroit, where I began to discover something very big and very wrong in my city and my country—white racism and the systemic segregation of our lives in the Motor City, including in the churches. Getting no answers in my home church to my questions about why white and black Detroit seemed so different, I went into the city and found some answers, including in the black churches.

I'll never forget a conversation with an elder in my Plymouth Brethren congregation worried about my interest in these questions. He told me, "Son, you need to understand that Christianity has nothing to do with racism; that's political, and our faith is personal." That was the moment I left my childhood and family faith, in my head and heart, and soon went on to join the social movements of my generation. I didn't have the words to put around that talk with the elder then but found them later after coming back to my faith after years of organizing—*God is personal, but never private.* The rest of my life and vocation has been to try to take personal faith public; faith can and should make a difference in the world.

Once again, Walter Brueggemann shows us what that means—to live in the world as persons of faith and to work with God to change it according to God's purposes.

Brueggemann begins by helping us understand how this problem started in the churches—not just mine. In the sixth century, a couple of centuries after the Roman emperor Constantine took over the early church, Christianity became much less concerned with the material well-being of its adherents and more otherworldly; and Brueggemann observes that this trend very much persists in wealthy churches today. Brueggemann says this understanding of material issues, as they actually affect the overwhelming majority of human beings who are not rich, is so bad that rich Christians are like "infants" in faith on matters of materiality. This is indeed behind some of the resistance to "getting political" in a way that would make rich churchgoers uncomfortable. This results in a church that is "weak or lacking in moral passion about the great issues of the day," he writes.

Brueggemann explains that the proper, originally intended, "material" aspect of faith is grounded in two factors: First, God created the world and called it good. Second, Jesus was God incarnated into the world and "went about doing good" of "a vigorously material kind," that is, healing the sick, telling good news to the poor, giving sight to the blind, and so forth.

Right from the start of this eloquently written volume, Brueggemann shows clearly that "materiality" should not be confused with "materialism." He then goes into five big areas of life where his "mature materiality" applies. These are some of the most provocative and creative essays on money, food, the body, time, and place that I have ever seen.

What struck me most was how these are the kind of teachings and learnings, pastoral conversations and care, and prophetic instruction about how to make a practical difference in the world that local congregations should be having among their parishioners, week in and week out. Now that would make a real difference in the world—and, in our local neighborhoods, people would notice this as both the "good life" and the "common good."

The first of the five main meditations is a perceptive and provocative analysis of the proper role of money in the life of a Christian. In the midst of our societal and political conversations about the bottom line, our paychecks, and the debates about structural and persistent and inequality, Brueggemann speaks to concrete things like earnings and investments and has particularly sharp words for those who conflate investment with labor—particularly those who elevate the former above the latter. As Brueggemann puts it, "It is an illusion to think that investment income is 'earned' or that it entails work." He goes on, "Our society has done almost nothing to guarantee or ensure just earning for so many." Earning, says Brueggemann, should be put in an entirely different context—that of community. "When earning is set within community, earning power, its expectations, its promise, and its restraints may take on a very different texture." More broadly, decisions around money present clear faith choices: "The great decision for materiality is to be a *contributor* to creaturely well-being or to be a *user* who diminishes and exhausts our common creatureliness."

Charity is not enough for us as people of faith. Brueggemann says, "Beyond charity, however, the great marker of saving the neighbor in the Bible concerns the regular cancellation of debt." True love for one's neighbor and care for the vulnerable should include the regular cancellation of debt, a theme woven strongly throughout Scripture. Even our most common prayer, the Lord's Prayer that Jesus taught us to pray, raises the practical issue of forgiving our debtors. Brueggemann zooms out and explains that this impulse toward debt cancellation derives from a very practical vision of economic justice: "The intent of these provisions is to preclude the formation of a permanent poverty class and to permit the disadvantaged to participate in a viable economic life."

Ultimately, the key to a healthy and holy economy is recognizing to Whom the world belongs. Brueggemann explains that since we have received and continue to receive the generous blessings of creation from our Creator, our response should be "glad generosity." The notion that any of us is "self-made or self-sufficient" is exposed as nonsense when we understand just how much we have always depended on our Creator's generous gifts.

Brueggemann even makes a compelling case for taxes! He explains the importance of good and just taxation for funding the common good of our communities and societies, while noting that Christians also have the obligation to oppose taxes levied to fund injustice or levied in an unjust manner. As he puts it, "Responsible materiality requires advocacy for good taxes that enhance the common good." For Brueggemann, the spending and taxation that occurs locally within communities is among the most important for promoting that common good. In his words, "Keeping money local is an important ingredient in mature materiality."

Brueggemann's meditation on money is not a pious conversation about the individuality of our spiritual lives and private economic existence. Rather, his observations—rooted in Scripture throughout—make connections between personal and communal financial decisions and arrangements connected to God's purposes in the world. He provides a moral and spiritual handbook for those "kitchen-table conversations" we hear so much about.

On the subject of food, Brueggemann's analysis is no less compelling. Whether the topic is food stamps for the poor, or life-saving global aid to the hungry, or diets for the wealthy who want to lose weight, or why people tell us "you are what you eat," or health and ecological concerns around fast foods and food waste, or why people should be vegetarians (or not), we think about and talk about food all the time. How does any of that have to do with God's purposes in the world or our responsibilities to each other or God's creation?

Again, Brueggemann puts this all into theological and biblical perspective, and where else can we find that?

The fundamental faith contrast, says Brueggemann, is between an economy of scarcity where there are winners and losers and an economy of abundance where there is always enough—if it is shared. As he puts it, "Jesus offers a contrast to *the practice of scarcity* for his disciples who are invited to *God's abundance*."

Brueggemann also speaks of "eating in companionship" instead of food consumption being such a private, secret, and guilty practice. He prophetically describes the injustice to the planet, the people, and all God's other creatures from industrial agriculture in contrast to smaller local production and eating, and says we should replace the "food chain" with a "food network." And all of that would build community.

In discussing the Christian relationship to the body, Brueggemann explains that the worship of God (as in Rom. 12) requires that "the bodily sacrifice" offered to God be "the self given over to the radical ethic of God's graciousness now enacted as graciousness toward the neighbor. We are a long way past preoccupation with self-care and with sexuality, though both *healthy self-care* and *healthy sexuality* are subsumed in this bodily sacrifice." This takes us deeper than the endless societal preoccupation with ourselves and our sexual success—which further isolates and separates us. Self-care is so much more than shopping; and sexuality is more than transactional but made for covenantal long-term commitment.

Our "body" is more than just our physical existence, but also our common identity. He says, "The mature materiality of the body, however, will transcend self-preoccupation to identify itself to be a part of the 'body politic.'" What Dr. Martin Luther King Jr. called "an inescapable network of mutuality" binds us together in a way that creates very real obligations toward each other, all of which carries political implications and responsibilities for being a good citizen.

Brueggemann also cites Ta-Nehisi Coates, describing how black bodies became "stolen bodies" in American history and how that was and continues to be a destruction of the body of Christ and an assault on the image of God from creation. To "perform the alternative world of the gospel," he says, requires "the practice of neighborliness."

He also takes on the subject most avoided by a culture that always wants to be young. Belief in the "Easter Christ" does indeed imply that we should not see our inevitable mortal death as the end, but that indeed the "illusion of immortality" is a creation of the consumer culture in order to extract resources from us by promising "that the next product will make us healthy, keep us young" as we attempt to "refuse our diminishment." "Finally," Brueggemann says, "indeed 'finally,' mature materiality lives in the awareness that we will die; our bodies (selves) are transient." Christians should prepare for "the dying of a good death" not in resignation, but in hope.

In addressing the subject of time, Brueggemann takes us beyond our private "rat race" schedules to an awareness that "our times are in God's hand." He says that Sabbath is the defining moment in all time. All six previous days of the week move toward Sabbath time. "It is so for the creation as it is for the creator (Gen. 2:1–4a)." He stresses the critical role of keeping Sabbath as the "refusal to have one's life defined by the production and consumption demands of a commoditized economy." In this way, keeping Sabbath is intrinsically an act of worship that proclaims God's lordship over commodity, production, schedule, and "the fatiguing world of things."

Brueggemann also offers a hopeful analysis of the famous Ecclesiastes 3:1–8 passage that begins, "For everything there is a season, and a time for every matter under heaven." In focusing on the pairing of that which is "plucked up" and that which is "planted," Brueggemann invites us to receive the hope that comes from time being in God's hands, without diminishing our responsibility to act in concert with God's purposes for the world: "It seems clear enough that the violent ideologies of race, class, gender, and white nationalism are under profound critique and assault. Conversely, we are witnessing the 'planting and building' of a new social world of multicultural openness that attests the love of neighbor toward those who happen to be different from us." In relaying this hopeful vision of the future, Brueggemann cites the Rev. Martin Luther King asking, "How long?" before asserting that "the arc of the moral universe is long, but it bends toward justice."

Brueggemann's final meditation in this book is on the subject of place. Place is central for the people of God, as shown by both the creation and the incarnation. Brueggemann says, "Mature materiality is invited to reflect on what it means to belong to a home place with all of its expectations, requirements, demands,

and gifts. Such reflection may also lead to fresh awareness of the cost of being without such a place, away
from home."

In his characteristic prophetic style, Brueggemann
takes the opportunity here to break down the roots
of homelessness in American society: "We not only
live in an economy that is *occupied by homeless persons*;
we live in an economy that is busy *producing homeless
persons.* The capacity to produce homeless persons is
deeply enmeshed in a privatized, greedy economy of
low wages, predatory loan arrangements, and regressive tax policy. It is easy enough, moreover, to imagine that much of our current homelessness is a residue
of slavery in which a population of laborers ended a
lifetime of work with no resources." In a similar vein,
Brueggemann exposes gentrification as "aggression"
that "puts vulnerable inheritance at risk." A mature
understanding of place requires "full commitment to
such regard for one's right place and equal regard for
the right place of the neighbor, including the vulnerable neighbor."

He also stresses the importance of place in provid-
ing roots, arguing that "everyone comes from somewhere. Everyone comes from a particular place with its
particular hope and particular resources and particular
social protocols and particular foods. These particulars may be amended and critiqued, but they cannot
be safely scuttled in a wholesale way for the sake of
rootless imagination. Thus the 'right place' to be is a
place that is infused with particulars that impose costs,
give gifts, and offer rootage. We are not meant to be
and finally cannot be rootless, placeless occupants of

'nowhere'; finally, we must be obligated, contributing partners in a time and place." That sense of partnership with our place is critical, rather than the all too prevalent notion of human ownership. Instead, "the owner is assigned to a purpose, not of maximizing production, but rather of enhancing the well-being of the home place." Brueggemann ties all this back to creation itself as "the place and the owner belong to each other and are cast together in a long-range destiny."

Walter Brueggemann's extraordinary book is very *this-worldly*; and that's why it is so important. This is reading and reflection for Sunday school classes, Bible study groups, good sermons, ecumenical gatherings, and faith-based organizing in all our communities. It is a must read for all of us who passionately but also practically want to participate in God's purposes for the world.

Jim Wallis

ACKNOWLEDGMENTS

I AM GRATEFUL TO JIM WALLIS FOR WRITING THE FORE-word for me. His whole life of testimony has been an exercise of mature materiality. I am, yet again, grateful to my friends at Westminster John Knox Press—David Dobson, Julie Tonini, David Maxwell, and their colleagues—and to Mark Price for writing the discussion questions. And I am most appreciative for the assistance of John Brueggemann, who helped bring this manuscript to completion.

INTRODUCTION

For though by this time you ought to be teachers, you need someone to teach you again the basic elements of the oracles of God. You need milk, not solid food; for everyone who lives on milk, being still an infant, is unskilled in the word of righteousness. But solid food is for the mature, for those whose faculties have been trained by practice to distinguish good from evil.

—Hebrews 5:12–14

IN THE EARLY CHURCH, CHRISTIAN CONGREGATIONS AND their bishops paid generous and deliberate attention to the plight of the poor and managed to give relief. In the sixth century (long after the much-maligned Constantine) there was a rather abrupt turn away from this attentiveness, as the church became *private* about wealth and *otherworldly* in its hope. The cause of this abrupt turn, Peter Brown has shown, was that the wealthy population became dominant in the church and did not want its wealth subject to the needs of the poor in the church.[1] This turn toward the private and otherworldly is evident, as Brown documents, first of all in the erection of grand mausoleums as hope for another life and as an ostentatious exhibit of wealth.

And second, there was an "othering" of the clergy, so that priests and bishops were distanced from "the real world" and assigned to be representatives of the sacred:

> Hence we witness a progressive "othering" of the clergy. They became a sacral class. Their dress, hair style, and sexual behavior were increasingly expected to be sharply different from that of the laity. Religious dress became sharply distinguished from lay dress. The tonsure was taken on as a sine qua non of both the clerical and the monastic state. It is notable that the origins of the tonsure did not lie in any clerical regulations. It came from the ground up. The cutting of hair (both of beards and of the top of the head) had long been treated by Romans as a sign of special dedication. The tonsure emerged as a response to lay demand for such a sign. Those who interceded for the laity, as a sacral class, were to be clearly designated by means of a ritual of shaving the crown of the head that had deep roots in the ancient folklore of hair.[2]

In effect the church gave up its preoccupation with material matters and became busy with spiritual matters of "soul-making" for the next world. That turn away from the material has continued in wealthy churches to this day, as is evidenced by the gentle admonition often made to pastors, "Don't become political." This familiar mantra of course is not against being "political," but only against the type of "political" that disturbs the comfort zone of the parishioner. It is much preferable to have the pastor confined to matters "sacral." (Shades of the sixth century!) The matter is very different in the churches of the poor that do not hesitate to address matters of materiality.

In the Epistle to the Hebrews, the writer generally appeals to the addressees of the letter with positive encouragement to greater faith and bolder testimony. In 5:12–14, however, the writer chides the addressees because they "refuse to grow up."[3] They continue to rely on "baby food" of the gospel and so wish to remain "infants" who lack skills to address urgent matters of good and evil. It is my thought that in the contemporary wealthy church (most of the Western church!), by happenstance or by intention many members remain "infants" in faith about matters of materiality. They prefer the "milk" and pabulum of a convenient, private, otherworldly gospel about "souls" rather than the solid food of informed critical thought about the materiality of our faith. As a consequence, much of the church is resistant to engagement in real-life material issues of faith and is quite content to settle for "innocent religion." And in much of this the pastors of the church collude because it often too hard and too risky to do otherwise. The result is a church that is weak or lacking in moral passion about the great issues of the day.

What follows here is a study of some of the dimensions of faith that are front and center when we consider the materiality of our faith. That material aspect of faith is grounded in our conviction about creation: the world is God's creation that God has called good. It is further grounded in our conviction concerning the incarnation, the confession that God has come bodied ("became flesh," John 1:14) in Jesus of Nazareth, who "went about doing good" (Acts 10:38) of a vigorously material kind:

The blind receive their sight, the lame walk, the lepers
are cleansed, the deaf hear, the dead are raised, the
poor have good news brought to them. (Luke 7:22)

That materiality performed by Jesus is not to be
confused with material*ism*, because the gospel accent
on the material is grounded in the conviction that the
truth of our life summons us to hope-filled obedience,
an obedience that is always referred back in gladness to
the goodwill of the creator God. Nobody called Jesus
a "materialist" because he healed the sick or brought
good Jubilee news to the poor. I judge that, after the
manner of his ministry, attention to the material
dimensions of our common life and our capacity for
critical, honest, faithful thought and action is urgent in
our cultural context.

I intend to suggest that the church, and most
particularly its leadership, have both an obligation
and an opportunity to reengage the materiality of
faith after a very long run of avoidance. In what
follows I explore aspects of our shared bodily existence wherein all of the gifts and tasks of evangelical
faith are deeply operative. I can readily think of five
dimensions of this materiality, and readers may think
of many others as well. The aim is that we may ingest
"solid food" and become more "mature," with skills
and faculties for moral thought and moral action in
the real world. I have no wish to deny the personal or
the otherworldly aspects of our faith, but I have no
doubt that redress about the centrality of the material
is urgent among us.

QUESTIONS FOR DISCUSSION

Walter Brueggemann's introduction issues this urgent invitation: "reengage the materiality of faith." His argument throughout the book is grounded in key assumptions he lays out in the introduction. In light of that, consider beginning your group's discussion with the following questions:

Brueggemann observes that by the sixth century, the church became preoccupied with "spiritual matters of 'soul-making' for the next world" (p. 2), as evidenced by buildings (grand mausoleums) and clergy (intentionally distinct from laity by dress and lifestyle).

– What evidence would you cite today that shows the church and its clergy remain primarily attentive to "spiritual" matters? What are the implications, either positive or negative, of that?

Brueggemann's understanding of "materiality" is grounded in theological convictions about creation and the incarnation (p. 3).

– How does the appeal to God's creation as good and Jesus' embodiment of doing good help clarify the meaning of the phrase "materiality of faith"?

Finally, as a way to help your group be clear from the outset about this notion of materiality, invite participants to think of other dimensions of it, in addition to the five discussed in the book (money, food, body, time, and place).

Chapter 1

MONEY*

Do not store up for yourselves treasures on earth, where moth and rust consume and where thieves break in and steal; but store up for yourselves treasures in heaven, where neither moth nor rust consumes and where thieves do not break in and steal. For where your treasure is, there your heart will be also.

—Matthew 6:19–21

AN OBVIOUS PLACE TO BEGIN CRITICAL REFLECTION ON THE materiality of our lives is with money. Money is a useful vehicle for the exchange of goods, a use that justifies market transactions. Money is, however, at the same time a powerful symbol (variously socially constructed) of influence, power, success, and virtue. It is to this latter function of money that material direction must attend, for in our society most of us are quite "innocent" about the spiritual propulsion of which money is capable.[1]

---

*For a more complete exposition of the theme of this chapter, see Walter Brueggemann, *Money and Possessions* (Louisville, KY: Westminster John Knox Press, 2016).

A Christian critical understanding of money might
begin with the dictum of John Wesley: *Earn all you can;
give all you can; save all you can.* This dictum reflects a
simple, responsible relationship to money. As we will
see, however, this seemingly simple statement covers
over a host of issues that will be usefully explored:

How much is enough to earn?
How little is enough to give?
How might one invest one's savings?

An effective way into these questions is to begin
as the Faith and Money Network (a satellite of the
Church of the Saviour in Washington, DC) regularly
began its seminars on money. The beginning point is to
have participants in the seminar tell, in as much detail
as possible, their personal story of money, how they
experienced money in their early family life, how that
family modeled money, and how the family earned,
saved, and shared its money.

These matters are complicated for members of our
society because a pervasive practice of consumerism,
enabled by a theory of capitalist privatism, treats money
as autonomous, as unrelated to the larger context of
society. And when money is treated autonomously, all
of the anchoring guidelines of Wesley are promptly
nullified. The outcome of such an unanchoring is that
money is valued instrumentally without reference to
social context and without any awareness of either the
gifts or the requirements of our social locations.

Consider first, *earn all you can.* Our capitalist society
is vexed by the Protestant work ethic of Max Weber,

whether or not there is in fact a connection to Calvin in our work ethic. There is no doubt that honest productive work is a virtue in our society, and it is rightly well paid . . . or should be. Thus the capacity to earn more by work is to be affirmed.

There are, however, a number of problems with Wesley's simple formula:

How much is enough? Is "enough" less than "all you can"? In a time of mobile capital and the technological capacity to accumulate endlessly, "all you can" has no limit or restraint. Work may become a passion and an end in itself, so that accumulation of wealth becomes an addiction that expels the human dimensions of our lives. On the one hand, is payment for honest, productive work different from investment income, contradicting the old TV ad about "making money the old-fashioned way," which meant managing one's investments wisely? It is an illusion to think that investment income is "earned" or that it entails work. Roland Boer points out that in the ancient world those who lived on surplus wealth were in fact "nonproducers":

> The system of estates sought to deal with a very practical matter: how does one feed and clothe the nonproducers? Or rather, how does one enable the nonproducing ruling class to maintain the life to which its members had quickly become accustomed? Directly or indirectly (via tenure), managed estates were the answer.[2]

Of course it is not different in our world, in which the "nonproducing ruling class" depends on the (poorly paid) work of others. We are wont, in our society, to regard the indigent and unemployed as the "nonproducers" when in fact the "nonproducers" include those who rely on surplus wealth and investment income for which "earning" is a misguided misnomer.

On the other hand, what of those who lack earning power? The Protestant work ethic has pertained primarily to white males in our society as the ones who by work gained the virtue of wealth and success. But of course most such high earners, from the outset, had unacknowledged advantages.[3] What of racial or ethnic minorities, women, the disabled, and especially those who carry the legacy of enslavement who never gain access to well-paid honest work? Our society has done almost nothing to guarantee or ensure just earning for so many. And for so many disinherited by our economy, their work is not adequately rewarded, so that honest work is not rightly well paid, rendering a viable life impossible. Conversely the well-connected high earners protect their edge through tax arrangements, legacy education, and other advantages that are denied those willfully left behind in our economy.

The work of mature materiality concerning "earn all you can" is to expose in critical ways the privatized, individualized notion of earning so that earners can begin to see themselves situated in a community of earners, some of whom enjoy huge advantage, some of whom are denied access, and all of whom are skewed by the pernicious norm of privatized wealth. When earning is set within community, earning power, its expectations, its promise, and its restraints may take on a very different texture.

Second, consider *save all you can*. Taken at its most simple, Wesley's guideline means to gather, store, and keep all the money you can. Taken in such a way, the phrase amounts to a welcome barrier against the creedal urging of consumerism, "Spend all you can." Thus in the first instant, the imperative is to resist the seductions of consumerism that more "things" will make us safe, happy, and better. Judging by the mass of TV ads, the great trifecta of well-being turns out to be more drugs, more new cars, and more electronic devices. Wesley's dictum invites resistance against these offers, an insistence that another drug, another new car, or another electronic device will not enhance our existence.

Mature materiality, however, will linger longer over the imperative verb, "save." Whatever Wesley intended, this verb of mandate must be taken more fully. A responsible practice of materiality might consider two other dimensions of saving. First, save the earth as our natural habitat. The earth is now being wasted and devastated by our industrial practice of excessive fossil-energy use coupled with a throwaway attitude toward consumer products. Mature materiality will usefully take a plunge into the inimitable work of Wendell Berry, our great apostle of frugality:

> We have only one choice. We must either properly care for all of it [nature] or continue our lethal damage to all of it.[4]

> In the age of industrialism, this relationship [of mutuality between nature and human beings] has been radically brought down to a pair of hopeless assumptions: that the natural world is passively subject either

to unlimited pillage as a "natural resource," or to par-
tial and selective protection as "the environment."[5]

We must achieve the character and acquire the skills
to live much poorer than we do.[6]

We are going to have to learn to give up things that we
have learned (in only a few years, after all) to "need."[7]

It is surely the duty of the older generation to be
embarrassingly old-fashioned.[8]

Such a saving is not storing up for one's self; it is
rather saving in a way that articulates our lives as a
part of a larger web of creaturely life to which we may
contribute. The great decision for materiality is to be a
contributor to creaturely well-being or to be a *user* who
diminishes and exhausts our common creatureliness.

Second, our mandate to "save all you can" means
to save our neighbors. In the Bible the "quadrilateral of
vulnerability" includes widows, orphans, immigrants,
and the poor (see Deut. 24:19–22), all those who have
no standing or leverage in a predatory patriarchal economy. Such saving would entail sustained acts of charity whereby the disadvantaged share in the wealth and
property of the community. Ownership is everything!
Beyond charity, however, the great marker of saving
the neighbor in the Bible concerns the regular cancellation of debt, and that in a society that willfully creates a debtor class in order to ensure a pool of cheap
labor! Thus Moses provides for a periodic cancellation
of debt in the "year of remission" (Deut. 15:1–18) and
a restoration of lost property in the practice of Jubilee
(Lev. 25). The Lord's Prayer, the one that Christians
pray most habitually, has at its center a petition for debt

forgiveness: "And forgive us our debts, as we also have forgiven our debtors" (Matt. 6:12).[9] The intent of these provisions is to preclude the formation of a permanent poverty class and to permit the disadvantaged to participate in a viable economic life.

Clearly "save all you can" draws energy away from a simple private accumulation of money to a wise deployment of money for the sake of the neighborhood and for a neighborly creation.

Third, *give all you can*. Responsible materiality depends upon glad generosity that is grounded in deep gratitude for the gift of life in all its abundance. In a society of competition among individuals for scarce goods, the pressure to get ahead is without restraint. But responsible materiality does not inhabit a world of scarce goods. Rather it resides in a creation of God's good abundance. Thus responsible materiality is exactly a contradiction to the impulse for competitive accumulation. The ground for generosity is the awareness that the world is funded by a generous, active God who has made creation as a gift that keeps on giving, and that we are on the receiving end of that endless gift-giving! Thus we need not and cannot imagine that we are self-made or self-sufficient. Nor does it follow that "I made my money and it belongs to me." Responsible materiality recognizes that we are each and all embedded in a life-giving network, and we are permitted the glorious chance to be full participants in and contributors to that life-giving network.

Three matters seem particularly important. In contemporary society we are very much prone to ad hoc practices of generosity (such as crowdfunding) in response to specific identifiable crises of need. That generosity is all to the good. It is, however, not sufficient for responsible materiality. Beyond ad hoc acts of giving, mature generosity requires planned, regular, disciplined budgeting for sustained giving. Such intentionality makes it possible not only to respond to dramatic crises but also to provide sustained support for social institutions upon which community health depends. The amount of such giving is flexible. We may note, however, that the notion of a 10 percent tithe of income is not a maximum; it is a baseline against which we may reckon our measure of generosity. Obviously the more we practice the restraints indicated above, the more we are able to maximize our generosity in a way commensurate with our gratitude.

Second, responsible Christian materiality has a great stake in the public good, the arena of neighborliness. Investment in the common good most often takes the form of tax payment. In a society of individual competitiveness, taxes are seen as a pernicious intrusion into one's monetized freedom that must be vigorously resisted and minimized. Such resistance is nothing less than a retreat from the common good. In Christian materiality, the payment of taxes is a form of giving back to the community that may be welcomed. Of course not all taxes are good or welcome. Some are ignoble and indeed are pernicious. Responsible materiality requires advocacy for good taxes that enhance the common good. These might include better funding for public schools, improved infrastructure that is available to all, and provision for essential food and housing. The need for good taxation in responsible materiality is underscored by Ariann. Huffington's observation that it is "much easier" to raise money for "the opera and fashionable museums than for at-risk children. . . . The task of overcoming poverty will not be achieved without the raw power of government appropriations."[10] Christian materiality does not shrink from the raw power of government and advocates its mobilization in the service of the common good. This form of giving is not only an act of generosity; it is also an act of good citizenship, even patriotism!

Third, in chapter 5 I exposit the importance of "place" for mature materiality. When we join our commitment to *place* to our management of *money*, it follows that monetary investment and expenditure should be focused locally to serve the neighborhood economy. It is crucial to "keep the money at home." Such a commitment tilts against unrestrained engagement with big-box stores and merchandising chains (notably those online) that intend to move the money out of the neighborhood. (An easy case to cite is the choice of a local bookstore over against the "convenience" of Amazon; extracting money from the local economy is characteristically "convenient"!) Keeping money local is an important ingredient in mature materiality.

This triad of *earning, saving,* and *giving* may lead to a repositioning of the monetized self in a network of neighborliness as a contributing member of the community. These three foci help us to see that our society's dominant narrative of money believes, against Christian materiality:

Earning is all for the self with an endless accumulation.
Saving is a private enterprise designed to enhance
    the autonomous self.
Giving is likely to be parsimonious and erratic.

Mature materiality summons us to a radical reloca-
tion of the self that includes a departure from the usual
assumptions of our society concerning money.

QUESTIONS FOR DISCUSSION

The Bible

Read aloud Matthew 6:19–21.

–   How does this biblical teaching address, critique,
    or inform our relationship with money?

The Book

Call attention to Brueggemann's mention of the Church
of the Saviour seminar on money (p. 8):

–   Invite participants to share, as much as they feel
    comfortable, their personal story of money, not-
    ing in particular how they experienced their fam-
    ily earning, saving, and sharing money.

John Wesley's familiar dictum, "Earn all you can;
give all you can; save all you can," provides the foundation for Brueggemann's remarks in this chapter. Say

aloud Wesley's statement and then ask the group to respond to these three questions:

- How much is enough to earn?
- How little is enough to give?
- How should one invest savings?

Our pervasive practice of consumerism, observes Brueggemann, views money as "autonomous, as unrelated to the larger context of society" (p. 8), thereby nullifying Wesley's guidelines. Explore this perspective and where you find evidence of this in our own consumerist habits:

Earn All You Can
- What factors (personal or societal) contribute to skewing the notion of earning all you can into an invitation to the limitless accumulation of wealth?
- What does it mean to set our "earning power, its expectations, its promise, and its restraints" (p. 10) within the context of community? How might seeing ourselves as part of a "community of earners" inform our earning practices?

Save All You Can
- What factors (personal or societal) make it difficult to resist our culture's urging to spend all you can?
- Brueggemann's broadened concept of saving leads to an invitation to "wise deployment of money for the sake of the neighborhood and for

a neighborly creation" (p. 13). How would that kind of deployment look? What changes would it call for in our saving practices?

Give All You Can

- What factors (personal or societal) make us prone to be generous in response to immediate need rather than generous out of gratitude for God's abundant gifts?
- Brueggemann states that mature materiality requires "planned, regular, disciplined budgeting for sustained giving" (p. 14) and "advocacy for good taxes that enhance the common good" (p. 14). Imagine incorporating those requirements into our giving practices; what challenges or opportunities might you expect?

Chapter 2

FOOD

"You give them something to eat." . . . *All ate and were filled; and they took up twelve baskets full of broken pieces and of the fish.*

—Mark 6:37–43

NOTHING IN OUR LIVES IS MORE IMMEDIATE AND CONSTANT than the requirement of food. Food is the most specific materiality that is before us daily. For that reason, mature materiality must address it and invite critical reflection on food. In the first instant, the concern is to eat "real food" that nourishes, to eat with mindfulness and restraint, and to maintain good weight and bodily health through food choices and exercise. That must be a major agenda in a society beset by junk food, eating disorders, disordered eating, and obesity.

Beneath that immediate concern about food, however, our deeper difficult question pivots around the issue of *scarcity and abundance*. That matter is made central in the parable of Luke 12:13–21. Jesus' story portrays a rich man, a rich farmer who specialized in accumulation, who strategized to store up more and more food (grain) because in his anxiety he imagined he did not have enough yet.[1] His appetite for more grain became insatiable. And his insatiability turned out to be lethal for him; he died in his "foolishness." He was a victim of imagined scarcity. He believed there was not enough, so he had to secure for himself much more than enough.

In the Gospel of Luke, the parable of Jesus revolves around a warning against greed (v. 15) that is then expanded by the instruction Jesus gives to his disciples in the next paragraph (vv. 22–31). Jesus offers a contrast to *the practice of scarcity* for his disciples who are invited to *God's abundance*. He witnesses to a trustworthy abundance that gives the lie to the scarcity imagined by the farmer in the parable. He summons his disciples out of the narrative of scarcity and into his alternative narrative of abundance. That abundance, Jesus attests, is grounded in the generative capacity of the creator God who supplies adequate food for birds, for lilies, and for those who "strive for God's kingdom" (v. 31), that is, a realm of justice, righteousness, and mercy. Thus the work of mature materiality concerning food is to move our mindfulness away from an imagined scarcity that evokes excessive accumulation and satiation to a trustworthy abundance that permits us to be free of worry about what we shall eat (v. 22).

It will be useful, in mature materiality, to reflect on the compelling power of the narrative of *scarcity.* For many in the "clean plate club," eating is required because of "starving children in Africa." Beyond that, however, is the relentless insistence of consumerism that we are entitled (because we are Americans) to have more and own more and eat more. The ideology of consumerism intends both (a) to affirm the legitimacy of satiation and (b) to attest that we do not yet have enough to be satiated and must still secure (purchase) the next offer of satiation.[2] The hope of mature materiality is that we may be disengaged from and resistant to that distortion of reality.

The ground for such disengagement and resistance is rooted in trust in the creator God and the generativity of God's creation that is the primary story line of the Bible. That biblical story line has its pivot point in the narrative of wondrous manna in Exodus 16. In that narrative Israel is in the wilderness, cut off from the food supply of Pharaoh. Very quickly the newly departed slaves, in their anxiety, yearn for Pharaoh's food supply (v. 3). In the wilderness there are no obvious life-support systems. In that very place that seems utterly bereft, however, bread is given . . . and meat . . . and water, all the necessities for life (Exod. 16:13, 15; 17:6; see Ps. 105:40–41)! A more mundane articulation of trust in abundance is offered by Wendell Berry in his characterization of Athey and Della Keith, who are the effortless practical embodiment of abundance:

> They were a sight to see, Della and Athey were, in their vigorous years. They had about them a sort of intimation of abundance, as though, like magicians, they might suddenly fill the room with potatoes, onions, turnips, summer squashes, and ears of corn drawn from their pockets. Their place had about it that quality of bottomless fecundity, its richness both in evidence and in reserve.[3]

It is clear, moreover, that in the "feeding miracles" of Jesus (Mark 6:30–44; 8:1–10) the wonder of manna bread in the wilderness is reiterated by Jesus, who feeds yet another hungry crowd in the wilderness. Where Jesus comes, there is ample bread, because Jesus embodies a life that is beyond the predatory reach of Pharaoh or Caesar!

In mature materiality it will be useful to trace the crisis of *scarcity/abundance* all through the process from farm to table. First, we may consider processes of food *production* around the question of scarcity and abundance. This issue comes down to a contrast between the family farm and industrial agriculture. It is not romantic to notice that food locally grown on family farms or through local gardening efforts sustained society for a long time. The industrial revolution, however, introduced more advanced technology and larger farm equipment that made it possible (and necessary?) for a single farmer to manage larger farming tracts. But of course investment in more costly equipment made it necessary to maximize production, and the maximization of production required the purchase of more acreage that in turn displaced the family farm. Production was further advanced by chemical fertilizers and by food cartels that control farm production through contractual arrangements and that have no interest in the farm, the land, the farmer, or even the quality of the food. The illusion of industrial agriculture is that such production could feed the world and indeed must feed the world, because the harvest of local efforts is taken to be too modest and therefore ineffective. The outcome is food that is "bechemicaled" (what a marvelous word!).

I like to eat vegetables and fruit that I know have lived happily and healthily in good soil, not the products of huge bechemicaled factory-fields that I have seen, for example, in the Central Valley of California. The industrial farm is said to have been patterned on the factory production line. In practice, it looks more like a concentration camp.[4]

A practical outcome of such practice is that farmers are at the mercy of uncaring food cartels and consumers are at the mercy of food chains that specialize in bechemicaled modes of food.

The alternative of the family farm offers better food:

Yes, in fact, small farms everywhere, in North America and also in the Third World, are more productive than large ones, for multiple reasons. An industrial soybean farm may produce more beans per acre, but the small farm, planted with six to twelve different crops, has a much higher yield, both in food quantity and in market value. Plants do favors for each other. In agrarian cultures in Mexico and northern Central America, farmers have traditionally interplanted "the three sisters": corn, beans, and squash. The corn provides trellises for the beans, the squash leaves discourage weeds and retard evaporation, and the beans fix nitrogen that enhances soil fertility for all three crops. Polycropping and even the planting of diverse varieties within a species also help with pest control; the different crops create more habitational niches for beneficial organisms, and harmful organisms are unlikely to have an equally devastating effect on every crop.[5]

Happily we are witnessing something of a disengagement from industrial agriculture. There is a new appreciation of the family farm; many younger farmers are willing and able to farm "small farms" without the industrial pressure to "get big or get out" (as US Agriculture Secretary Ezra Taft Benson urged farmers in the 1950s). There is also new energy in gardening (given some extra impetus by Michelle Obama). In my church congregation, for example, a community garden in the last year produced more than four thousand pounds of vegetables. The sale of this produce generated important income for the care and feeding of economically isolated persons.

Mature materiality will lead us to pay much greater attention to the modes of food production in which we participate by our choices of foods and our practices of eating. If we are in thrall to a notion of scarcity, we may embrace industrial production on the assumption that greater productivity will overcome scarcity. If, however, we are alive to God's abundance we may have confidence that land, respected and wisely cared for, will produce the local food that is required.

Second, we may consider the processes of food *distribution*. When food is grown locally, it will most naturally be delivered locally. Such local distribution makes it possible for consumers to deal directly with local producers. Locally grown food, moreover, is much more likely to be marked by compassionate neighborliness wherein food is more generously shared with neighbors who may lack resources or purchasing power. Such distribution readily becomes a practice of genuine neighborliness.

Our primary modes of food distribution wholly lack such a compassionate sensibility. In the pressured world of industrial production, distribution follows the familiar trajectories of wealth and poverty. As a result, those with great resources are able to enjoy vast accumulations of rich food. Such a capacity for accumulation is evident in the Bible when Pharaoh deprives the peasants in his domain of their means of production (Gen. 47:16–17). Consequently food distribution depends upon a food czar (Joseph the Israelite!) to mete out food according to the whim of Pharaoh. Pharaoh's practice of keeping surplus food for himself, moreover, is replicated by his son-in-law King Solomon, who enjoyed a lavish table that featured a vast inventory of meats, the very food denied to the peasants:

> Solomon's provision for one day was thirty cors of choice flour, and sixty cors of meal, ten fat oxen, and twenty pasture-fed cattle, one hundred sheep, besides deer, gazelles, roebucks, and fatted fowl. (1 Kgs. 4:22–23)

This extravagant surplus of food depended on the productivity of agrarian peasants who worked the soil for subsistence income. At the same time, this royal practice denied to those same peasants any access to such an extravagant diet.

It is easy enough to transpose that dramatic inequality in food distribution in the Bible to our own contemporary food distribution. In our practice, the wealthy can enjoy an abundance of lavish foods while subsistence workers (on a very low minimum wage) and others who are "left behind" get the leftovers from such distributive practices. This arrangement of food distribution is reflected in the parsimonious practice of

"food stamps" that is a grudging policy of food distribution. And now the imposition of work requirements
on the hungry reflects the dread of some wealthy that
"some needy person might get something for nothing"
from our vast abundance of food! The imposition of
work requirements on the vulnerable is matched by
generous government grants designed for the most
advantaged producers! That intentional inequity that
happens daily in our society occurs on international
scale as food becomes a weapon for the rich nations
against the poorer nations. Food becomes an instru-
ment of manipulation and extortion.

That inequitable practice of food distribution calls
to mind the parable of Jesus concerning a rich man
and Lazarus, who "longed to satisfy his hunger with
what fell from the rich man's table" (Luke 16:21).[6]
The parable proposes that the rich man and his ilk are
held to the demanding expectations of the Torah while
Lazarus is embraced by Father Abraham, a stand-in for
God's compassion. The parable suggests that parsimonious food distribution leads to an alienation that does
not and cannot come to a good end, while the tilt of
God's rule is toward those who hunger and are eventually blessed.

In the Gospel of Luke, it is affirmed that in God's
rule food distribution is radically different. Thus in the
opening manifesto of Mary, the mother of Jesus anticipates a radical redistribution of food:

> He has filled the hungry with good things,
> and sent the rich away empty.
>
> Luke 1:53

The song of Mary sets the tone for how Jesus is articulated by Luke. In Luke's version of Jesus' Beatitudes, Jesus anticipates a radical reversal of food distribution:

> Blessed are you who are hungry now,
> for you will be filled.
> . . . .
> Woe to you who are full now,
> for you will be hungry.
>
> Luke 6:21, 25

It is important to recognize that the transition from "now" to "time to come" in fact presents two competing narratives of well-being. Brooks Harrington has clearly seen that the contrast of "now" and "later" does not concern a coming never-never land.[7] Rather these two modes of distribution are both operative now and in contradiction to each other. It is the work of mature materiality to help us resituate ourselves in the face of that contradiction and to embrace, as fully as we are able, an alternative practice of food distribution congruent with the abundance of creation.

Third, mature materiality will invite fresh reflection on food *consumption.* Our current consumerism defines individual persons in our society as "consumers," as those who have both a right and an obligation to consume, to eat, to devour, to own, to occupy, to accumulate, to store up. Consumerism takes the world as an object that is available for full use and exploitation by human "masters."[8] It is, moreover, taken to be an inexhaustible resource, so that we as "masters" are free to use and eat without restraint or limitation. This is most evident in our consumption of fossil fuel for the sake of indulgence and "national defense" that, according to dominant national capitalism, must not be limited in any way. Indeed, we have arrived at a tacit agreement that consideration of the environment that in any way limits economic growth is illicit. An outcome of that passionate commitment to uncurbed consumption is that we get industrial food that is beset with chemicals that do damage to consumers as industrial production does damage to the soil. Such an ideology of consumption causes us to reperform endlessly the tale of Lazarus and the rich man. There can be no curb on consumption for those who have leverage and resources.

Mature materiality will invite our growth toward our personal reidentification so that we no longer understand ourselves as consumers who are authorized (and required!) to consume in uncurbed ways. Mature materiality may offer two alternative identities to us. First, we may grow into an identity as *citizens and members of the community*. That identity, on the one hand, means that our consumption of food is always with and in the company of other members of the community. Eating in companionship with the economically isolated may cause us to think differently about extravagance and indulgence that is in stark contrast to the eating prospects of our economically isolated neighbors. (The term *isolated* is used to indicate that the problem we readily label as "poverty" is the result of being cut off from economic resources that are necessary to live a viable life in our society. The phrase *economically isolated* is preferable to *poor* because it points to the systemic causes of such a condition.) As citizens we never eat alone, in isolation, but always with our neighbors who are present at the table with us or who await an invitation to the table with us. On the other hand, identity as citizens specifies that we have an obligation to participate in the formation of food policy and practice that impinges on local possibilities. Such an obligation may lead to engagement with lobbying efforts for policy, such as Bread for the World, an enterprise that aims to redefine policy and practice toward a more equitable distribution of food.

A second identity toward which we may grow through mature materiality is to accept ourselves as *creatures of God* along with other creatures of God. This will cause us to be aware that we are a part of not only a *food chain* but also a *food network* in which all creatures are entitled to adequate food. Our role as creatures, according to the Bible, is to "till" and "keep" the earth (Gen. 2:15), that is, to cultivate and preserve the earth as the giver of food in abundance. When we eat alongside other creatures and when we take responsibility for the entire network of eating creatures, we may consider our consuming habits very differently.

It is the aim of mature materiality to invite an intentional and disciplined regard for food that is fully attentive to the entire food process of *production*, *distribution*, and *consumption*. In such an awareness, there need be no more selfish "innocent" accumulation of food, for now food takes on marking as a sacramental process. Food is a sign of the generous abundance of the giving creator. Given that awareness, we are more fully prepared

to resist agricultural industrialization and its accompanying chemicals,

to resist privilege and entitled access to food for the
powerful and wealthy,
to resist ideologies of indulgent domination.

For these reasons, table prayers (as both affirmation and resistance) are compellingly appropriate. Such
prayers constitute a powerful act of gratitude, acknowl-
edging before we eat that food is a gift that must be
received in ways congruent with the God who gives
food. In the book of Psalms we are offered two table
prayers that fully recognize God as source of our food:

> These all look to you
> to give them their food in due season;
> when you give it to them, they gather it up;
> when you open your hand, they are filled with good
>   things.
>
> Ps. 104:27–28

> The eyes of all look to you,
> and you give them their food in due season.
> You open your hand,
> satisfying the desire of every living thing.
>
> Ps. 145:15–16

These utterances are recognitions that food is not produced by us; it is not to be distributed according to our
entitlements or appetites; and it is not to be consumed
with indifferent self-indulgence. Our prayers of gratitude affirm that we eat *in the presence of the God* who
gives bread to the eater and *in the presence of the neighbors* whom God loves as God loves us.

We have no better articulation of this pause of gratitude than the hymn of Matthias Claudius:

We plow the fields and scatter the good seed on the
        land,
but it is fed and watered by God's almighty hand;
he sends the snow in winter, the warmth to swell the
        grain,
the breezes and the sunshine, and soft refreshing rain.

All good gifts around us are sent from heaven above;
then thank the Lord, O thank the Lord for all his love.

He only is the Maker of all things near and far;
he paints the wayside flower, he lights the evening
        star;
the winds and waves obey him, by him the birds are
        fed;
much more to us, his children, he gives our daily
        bread.

We thank thee, then, O Father, for all things bright
        and good,
the seedtime and the harvest, our life, our health, our
        food;
the gifts we have to offer are what thy love imparts,
but chiefly thou desirest our humble, thankful hearts.[9]

The hymn begins with recognition of the human work of food production: plowing and scattering seed. But it turns then quickly away from human effort to divine generosity. The refrain affirms that "all good gifts" (surely the gift of food) are solely from God. Our only adequate response is thanks. Imagine *production* shaped by *thanks*! And *distribution* administered with *thanks*! And *consumption* paced by *gratitude*! The prayers and the hymn constitute pauses that gladly recognize God's generosity. In our most mature materiality, our *gratitude* may match God's *generosity*. The greed system of accumulation robs food of its sacramental potential. We should not then be surprised that we are left unsatisfied by food that cannot meet our creaturely hunger.

QUESTIONS FOR DISCUSSION

The Bible

Read aloud Mark 6:37–44

- How does the story of Jesus feeding the multitude address, critique, or inform how you understand and relate to food?

Read aloud Luke 12:13–24.

- How does Brueggemann's assessment of the rich farmer as a "victim of imagined scarcity" (p. 20) address our practices of acquiring and consuming food?

The Book

Brueggemann contrasts consumerism's narrative of scarcity with the Bible's story of trust in the abundance of God's creation:

- In what ways do the Old Testament stories of manna in the wilderness and the Gospel stories of Jesus' feeding miracles challenge our trust in our consumer habits?

- In what ways do our consumer habits undermine our trust in the biblical story line?

In addressing the food dimension of the materiality of faith, Brueggemann traces what he calls the "crisis of *scarcity/abundance*" through the process from farm to table (p. 22). Use the three parts of that process to guide the group's discussion:

Food Production

- To what extent do our food choices and eating practices reflect our uncritical trust of the commercial/industrial food production chain?
- What assumptions support confidence in a large-scale food production process to overcome fears of scarcity?
- What assumptions support confidence in God's abundance as an assurance against fears of scarcity?

Food Distribution

- What examples in our communities today reveal how surplus food available to those who can afford it is *not* available to those who cannot afford it?
- In what places and in what circumstances do you witness food distribution used as a weapon or as a means of extortion?
- How might Mary's song in Luke 1 and Jesus' teachings in Luke 6 encourage us as a Christian community to seek ways to participate in more equitable food distribution?

Food Consumption

- If a more faithful way of consuming food is, first of all, to stop seeing ourselves eating only as *consumers*, how do we do that? What keeps us from doing that?
- When we eat, we can identify as *citizens* (of a community). How would identifying ourselves in this way challenge or inform our eating practices?
- When we eat, we can identify as *creatures* (of God). How would identifying ourselves in this way challenge or inform our eating practices?

Close by praying together the hymn "We Plow the Fields and Scatter" (p. 31).

.

Chapter 3

THE BODY

For life is more than food, and the body more than clothing.
—Luke 12:23

MATURE MATERIALITY MUST FOCUS ON A MATURE SENSE OF the human body (Heb. *nephesh*). Jesus' statement to his disciples about the importance of life and body in Luke 12:23 follows the parable in which the rich farmer thinks his life consists in the accumulation of food; perhaps he cared more for his clothing and his appearance than he did for his body. The disciples of Jesus are to have their priorities straight. *Food and clothing* do not count for as much as *life and body.*

We may recognize at the outset that mature materiality concerning the body begins with responsible self-care. We know the routines and rules for responsible self-care: proper eating, proper exercise, and proper sleep, disciplines that refuse overeating, excessive passivity, and excessive restlessness. Good self-care does not specialize in drugs, cosmetics, excessive pursuit of consumer goods, or excessive online time that may detract from a centered self. We also know that social connectedness to neighbors makes for a healthy self in a healthy body. Mindfulness about responsible self-care matters centrally for mature materiality.

And of course mature materiality includes a healthy sense of and practice of sexuality that precludes both puritanical reluctance and promiscuous self-indulgence. Healthy sexuality is not preoccupied with technique or genitalia but with faithfulness in relationship. It is for that reason that the prophetic tradition of Israel, when it wants to reach into the depths of God's life with Israel, appeals to the imagery of marital commitment. No other relationship bespeaks God's passionate commitment to God's people as does the intensity of husband and wife. Thus in Hosea, God affirms to Israel:

> I will take you for my wife forever; I will take you for my wife in righteousness and in justice, in steadfast love, and in mercy. I will take you for my wife in faithfulness; and you shall know the LORD. (Hos. 2:19–20)

This "wedding vow" includes the five most central terms of covenantal fidelity in the biblical vocabulary. That same imagery is utilized in the Epistle to the Ephesians to characterize Christ's love for the church as one of self-giving, self-sacrificial fidelity:

> Husbands, love your wives, just as Christ loved the church and gave himself up for her. (Eph. 5:25)

That imagery, moreover, is inscribed in the singing of the church:

> From heaven he came and sought her to be his holy
>   bride.
> With his own blood he bought her, and for her life he
>   died.[1]

That imagery, of course, reflects an old patriarchal notion of male initiative and domination in a mutual relationship, a reflection that is altogether regrettable and obsolete.[2] Nevertheless, the reiterated use of the metaphor is worth noting, for the imagery reflects self-giving sacrificial fidelity of the deepest kind. That such imagery is subject to distortions of violence and abuse does not finally vitiate the positive force of the imagery in the imagination of ancient Israel.[3]

When our mature understanding of sexuality is cast in terms of long-lasting, self-giving fidelity, we are greatly distanced from much of what passes for sexuality in its commoditized forms in our society. Nadia Bolz-Weber has it just right in speaking of a "sexual reformation" away from the traditional shame that invites hiddenness and then exploitation and subjugation.[4] Such a "reformation," moreover, may deliver us from what my friend Joe Maguire, a Roman Catholic moral theologian, calls "pelvic theology," in which we are preoccupied with genitalia, while completely disregarding the relational matter of mutual fidelity. The "pelvic" theology of the church—with its aversion to gay persons—when we think about it, belongs in the same world as the puerile enjoyment of scatological humor by young boys, a puerile preoccupation extended in teen hookup culture and in adult pornography and then into the extremities of sex traffic that is remote from any thought of relational fidelity.[5] Maturity is an awareness that the capacity for long-term commitment is what matters and what is most richly expressed in healthy sexuality.[6]

Bodily maturity goes well beyond the obvious matters of *self-care* and *sexuality*. We may begin with the urgent imperative of Paul:

> I appeal to you therefore, brothers and sisters, by the mercies of God, to present your bodies as a living sacrifice, holy and acceptable to God, which is your spiritual worship. (Rom. 12:1)

Paul utilizes the vocabulary of temple worship concerning an offering that is acceptable to God. Such an offering traditionally might have been an animal sacrifice, or in a monetized culture, an adequate church pledge. Paul, however, transformed the legacy of sacrifice to "your bodies," the complete persons who have signed on with the gospel for life in the "coming age" of God's kingdom.[7] Thus the human body, that is, the whole person, is summoned to new behavior that is congruent with the new rule of God.

What follows in Romans 12 is an inventory of what the new behavior in the kingdom of God might look like. It is clear that Paul is not envisioning a dualism of body over against spirit, as verse 1 concludes with reference to "spiritual worship." Thus the *"body" (whole person)* offers *"spiritual worship."* But as N. T. Wright makes clear, the word rendered "spiritual" here could be better translated as "reasonable," so that Paul proposes that "the offering of the *body* is precisely the thing that *thinking* creatures ought to recognize as appropriate."[8] Wright's phrase "thinking creatures" obviously refers to those who are mature in faith and mature about the meaning and investment of their bodies. "Thinking persons" who yield reasonable bodily sacrifice are not calculating pragmatists. They are rather those whose lives are fully committed to the radical reign of Christ that Paul subsequently lines out in this chapter. Thus mature materiality focuses on the *new behavior* appropriate to the *new regime.*

As a result, mature materiality concerning the body consists in generosity, diligence, compassion, and cheerfulness (v. 8), genuine love (v. 9), mutual affection (v. 10), hope, patience, and perseverance in prayer (v. 12), hospitality (v. 13), harmonious living and association with the lowly (v. 16), peaceableness (v. 18), rejection of vengeance (v. 19), and generosity toward one's enemies (v. 20). This remarkable list of practices, taken to be quite ordinary for those embedded in God's grace about which Paul has written, quite frontally contradicts the way of the world. The mature body is put to different use! Thus the bodily sacrifice offered to God is the self given over to the radical ethic of God's graciousness now enacted as graciousness toward the neighbor. We are a long way past preoccupation with self-care and with sexuality, though both *healthy self-care* and *healthy sexuality* are subsumed in this bodily sacrifice. We are able to see that the ethic sketched out here is variously reiterated in the epistles of the New Testament that follow the book of Romans, both those of Paul and the General Epistles.

This bodily sacrifice is nothing less than a resitua-
tion of the self that is marked in the sacramental life of
the church by baptism.[9] Thus in the later Epistle to the
Ephesians we surely are offered a baptismal formula
for a new self newly clothed:

> You were taught to put away your former way of life,
> your *old self*, corrupt and deluded by its lusts, and to
> be renewed in the spirit of your minds, and to clothe
> yourselves with the *new self*, created according to the
> likeness of God in true righteousness and holiness.
> (Eph. 4:22–24; italics added)

As a result *the re-situated self* puts the ways of the *old
self* away:

> But fornication and impurity of any kind, or greed,
> must not even be mentioned among you, as is proper
> among saints. Entirely out of place is obscene, silly,
> and vulgar talk; but instead, let there be thanksgiving.
> (Eph. 5:3–4; see 4:31; Col. 3:5–14)

The practical mandate of which the new self is fully
capable follows:

> Be kind to one another, tenderhearted, forgiving one
> another, as God in Christ has forgiven you. (Eph. 4:32)

The contrast of *old self (body)* and *new self (body)*
is cast in the Letter to the Galatians as "works of the
flesh" and "fruit of the Spirit":

> Now the works of the flesh are obvious: fornication,
> impurity, licentiousness, idolatry, sorcery, enmities,
> strife, jealousy, anger, quarrels, dissensions, fac-
> tions, envy, drunkenness, carousing, and things like
> these. . . . By contrast, the fruit of the Spirit is love,

joy, peace, patience, kindness, generosity, faithfulness, gentleness, and self-control. (Gal. 5:19–23)[10]

Paul summarizes the new life of the newly bodied self:

> For the whole law is summed up in a single commandment, "You shall love your neighbor as yourself." . . . Bear one another's burdens, and in this way you will fulfill the law of Christ. (Gal. 5:14; 6:2)

The bodily self that offers "spiritual worship" is the self given over to the well-being of the neighbor. Thus the mature body is in contrast to the former self that lives only for the self. Both self-care and sexuality are readily recharacterized by this understanding of the mature self.

The mature materiality of the body, however, will transcend self-preoccupation to identify itself to be a part of the body politic. The notion of "body politic" sees that the corporate life, the life of the public economy, and the reality of law and policy together constitute an arena in which the mature body participates as a responsible citizen. Unfortunately too much Christian spirituality is highly privatized, whereas healthy spirituality propels one into active engagement in the public domain.

As a result the mature bodied self becomes aware of the ways in which policy and public practice impinge upon the personal well-being of one's self and one's neighbor. Consequently one develops a capacity to "follow the money" and to see how the power of money, for good or for ill, crowds in on personal lives. This in turn leads to a capacity to recognize the crucial public issues that concern the rule and will of

God, all of which have to do with the well-being of the neighbor and the viability of the neighborhood. The immature self is too often coddled by the church and remains excessively innocent about systems of power and excessively passive about the way in which law, policy, and corporate power may distort human personality or the ways in which law, policy, and corporate power may function in the service of the common good. In our society, the matter of distortion or benefit to the common good is very often articulated as "the American Dream," a Dream that has a complex and tenuous linkage to Christian faith.

We have no more searing exposition of the American Dream than that of Ta-Nehisi Coates. He sees the immense effort put into the maintenance of that Dream, now popularized by the slogan "Make America Great Again":

> But a very large number of Americans will do all they can to preserve the Dream. No one directly proclaimed that schools were designed to sanctify failure and destruction. But a great number of educators spoke of "personal responsibility" in a country authored and sustained by criminal irresponsibility. The point of this language of "intention" and "personal responsibility" is broad exoneration. Mistakes were made. People were enslaved. We meant well. We tried our best. "Good intention" is a hall pass through history, a sleeping pill that ensures the Dream.[11]

> The Dream thrives on generalization, on limiting the number of possible questions, on privileging immediate answers. The Dream is the enemy of all art, courageous thinking, and honest writing.[12]

Coates sees that the Dream has turned out to be a fiction that serves particular interests, even while the rhetoric seduces others in loyalty to it:

> The Dream seemed to be the pinnacle, then—to grow rich and live in one of those disconnected houses out in the country, one of those small communities, one of those cul-de-sacs with its gently curving ways, where they staged teen movies and children built tree-houses, and in that last lost year before college, teen-agers made love in cars parked at the lake.[13]

Coates then draws the Dream toward the reality of racist America:

> A legacy of plunder, a network of laws and traditions, a heritage, a Dream, murdered Prince Jones as sure as it murders black people in North Lawndale with frightening regularity. "Black-on-black crime" is jargon, violence to language, which vanishes the men who engineered the covenants, who fixed the loans, who planned the projects, who built the streets and sold red ink by the barrel. And this should not surprise us. The plunder of black life was drilled into this country in its infancy, and reinforced across its history. . . . The Dream of acting white, of talking white, of being white, murdered Prince Jones as sure as it murders black people in Chicago with frightening regularity.[14]

I have included this much from Coates because "innocent" Christianity, often preoccupied with spiritual matters, has not developed a capacity to honestly assess the continuing brutal bodily reality of the public domain that is a concern of the mature self. Coates draws his analysis very close to our theme of the body:

At the onset of the Civil War, our stolen bodies were worth four billion dollars, more than all of American industry, all of American railroads, workshops, and factories combined, and the prime product rendered by our stolen bodies—cotton—was America's primary export. The richest men in America lived in the Mississippi River Valley, and they made their riches off our stolen bodies. Our bodies were held in bondage by the early presidents. Our bodies were traded from the White House by James K. Polk. Our bodies built the Capitol and the National Mall. The first shot of the Civil War was fired in South Carolina, where our bodies constituted the majority of human bodies in the state. Here is the motive for the great war. It's not a secret.[15]

This brutal confiscation of bodies of course does not end with the Emancipation Proclamation.[16] We witness its continuation all around us in police brutality, rigged financial arrangements, and voter suppression. Contemporary bodies as "living sacrifices" in "spiritual worship" will have none of this continuation of "body snatching" that is so deep in our body politic. Bodies offered to God in "spiritual worship" not only will not participate in this brutality but will engage in active resistance and transformation of institutions and policies that make such modes of the Dream still much too credible. Mature bodies inescapably collide with the Dream. They engage in the day-to-day tedium of neighbor care, insisting that the Dream must be radically revised and edited. That revision cannot happen until there is lively awareness about the long history of body snatching as a dimension of the Dream that persists even now.

It is a present, even urgent, question, then, of how to find standing ground and sustaining companions that make possible the long, arduous work of transformative resistance to body snatching as common practice and ordinary policy. The answer given in the church, of course, is *the body of Christ* that characteristically has a tense relationship with *the body politic*. The notion of the church as the body of Christ is a daring but pervasive metaphor in the New Testament:

> So we, who are many, are *one body in Christ*, and individually we are members one of another. (Rom. 12:5; italics added)

> And he has put all things under his feet and has made him the head over all things for *the church, which is his body*, the fullness of him who fills all in all. (Eph. 1:22–23; italics added)

> . . . to equip the saints for the work of ministry, for building up *the body of Christ*. (Eph. 4:12; italics added)

> . . . just as Christ does for the church, because we are *members of his body*. (Eph. 5:29–30; italics added)

The image of body suggests that the community of believers is an active organism of complex parts, all of which are interconnected into a functioning living agency. On the one hand, Christ as the "head of the body" means that Jesus does the thinking for the body, that is, provides the guidance and assurances that define the body. On the other hand, the members of the body, enumerated as bodily parts, are interconnected and depend on each other for vitality and effectiveness.

Such imagery refuses the mistake that so besets much *Protestant privatism*, in which it is all about "me and Jesus," as if other congregants as well as other neighbors had no significance for "my faith." The imagery of "the body of Christ" at the same time refuses the *institutional reductionism* of the organized church that imagines that rules, protocols, and organizational charts constitute the character of the church. Such reductionism leads to struggles for authority and eventually to "guidelines" in the service of an imagined certitude. Against such a temptation, the image of "body" means that all members, even "lesser members," are essential to the full functioning of the body in response to its head. The claim is that we belong to each other, thus another dimension of the same fidelity that we have noted in our discussion of sexuality.

This declaration concerning "the body" in the several epistles voices the character of the church as an assemblage of interrelated members who are connected to each other, who rely on each other, who have the capacity to "speak the truth in love" to each other (Eph. 4:15).[17] As the epistles develop, however, it is clear that this body does not exist for its own well-being. It exists to act out and perform the alternative world of the gospel in the practice of neighborliness that contradicts the anti-neighborliness of the old order. This body is fully committed to the work of Christ, relies on Christ, and is sustained by Christ. Dietrich Bonhoeffer asks, "How then do we come to participate in the body of Christ, who did all this for us? . . . The answer is, through the two sacraments of His Body, baptism and the Lord's Supper."[18]

The sacramental portrayal of that bodily solidarity is in the Eucharist, wherein the members of the body regularly receive the sign and the reality of the body of Christ (Matt. 26:26; 1 Cor. 11:24). Bieler and Schottroff have written a most compelling exposition of the Eucharist as an act of eschatological imagination in which we eat into Christ's future that takes seriously the bodily reality of it: "Eschatological imagination is a practice of hope that encompasses a deep listening to the vulnerable voices that confront poverty and the destruction of life-sustaining resources."[19]

Paul's instruction for the Eucharist is to continue it "until [the Lord] comes" (1 Cor. 11:26). This is a meal of anticipation that voices readiness to leave behind the old failed world in recognition of the new world of resurrected life. Clearly that anticipatory accent has been lost in much of the church, but mature materiality will recover it. The structure of "then/soon" portrays the struggle for the future in which the communicant is prepared to participate:

> Jesus . . . knows about the struggle for the bread of life in the midst of these two economies. Issues of poverty and property threaten and challenge the Eucharistic life and affect the way the holy meal is celebrated.
>
> . . . The terrain of the *Homo oeconomicus* is the market exchange in which goods are exchanged for money. That exchange produces abstract relations between producers and consumers, relations not based on fulfillment of the basic needs of the individual or the community but on the multiplication and accumulation of money. . . .
>
> . . . We will seek to discover in the holy meal practices implicit alternatives to the logic assumed by the *Homo oeconomicus* theory. These alternative practices

may disrupt the worldview that market exchange logic is the only rational or "natural" way of engaging in economic affairs. Paying attention to the different forms of economic imagination the two economies provide will help deepen our understanding of sacramental permeability with regard to economic exchange and Eucharist.[20]

The Eucharist as eschatological imagination contradicts the claims of market ideology; for that reason bread is received differently.[21] It is broken and shared. (The contrast is bread that is *unbroken* and *unshared*.) This blest broken bread is eaten in anticipation of a future that embodies all those who are broken, all those who share in the inexplicable gift of life. Participation in the "broken body" is ground for resistance to the old world of private bread.[22]

Finally, indeed "finally," mature materiality lives in the awareness that we will die; our bodies (selves) are transient. The illusion of immortality in our culture is sustained (and required!) by the expectation that the next product will make us healthy, keep us young, and refuse our diminishment. Mature materiality is under no such illusion and prepares for the dying of a good death. Such preparation, however, is not resignation. It is rather an act of hope, for mature materiality lives in anticipation of the resurrection of the body after the manner of the Easter Christ. Mistaken spirituality has led to the seduction of immortality, the idea that there is something about us that does not die. Buoyant faith trusts otherwise; it affirms that the giver of broken bread is the Lord of life and the Lord of our futures. Mature materiality engages in an "as if," as if the kingdom of

God is "at hand," already present and operative among us (Mark 1:14–15).

QUESTIONS FOR DISCUSSION

The Bible

Brueggemann cites a number of Scripture passages in this chapter; a key text is Paul's appeal to the imagery of temple worship in Romans 12 as a way to imagine how believers embody kingdom of God behavior. Read chapter 12 aloud, then follow up with discussion:

– Where do you see examples of the practices of bodily sacrifice Brueggemann summarizes from Romans 12:8–20 opposing the practices of the world today? (See p. 39.)

Read these Scripture passages aloud in sequence: Ephesians 4:22–24; Ephesians 5:3–4; Colossians 3:5–14; Galatians 5:19–23.

– How do these passages help clarify Paul's notion in Romans 12 of faith as a bodily sacrifice?

The Book

Brueggemann states that mature materiality concerning the body includes responsible care of the self and covenantal practice of sexuality, and that "both *healthy self-care* and *healthy sexuality* are subsumed" in Paul's call for an ethic based on the metaphor of bodily sacrifice.

  – Where and in what ways do you see *healthy self-care* acted out (or not) in the life of the Christian community today?
  – Where and in what ways do you see *healthy sexuality* acted out (or not) in the life of the Christian community today?
  – How can Romans 12:1 provide a vision of the blessings and boundaries of both healthy self-care and healthy sexuality?

"The mature bodied self becomes aware of the ways in which policy and public practice impinge upon the personal well-being of one's self and one's neighbor" (p. 41).

  – What policies in our community are critiqued by mature materiality of the body?
  – What public practices in our community are critiqued by mature materiality of the body?

Brueggemann offers an extensive critique of the ideal of the American Dream as it relates to the reality of racism in America. He cites the work of Ta-Nehisi Coates as a way of connecting the theological metaphor of the body with those actual bodies "snatched" by the practices of racial injustice, past and present.

  – How does Brueggemann's use of the twin metaphors—Paul's *bodily sacrifice* and Coates's *body snatching*—inform our understanding of what constitutes "spiritual worship" (Rom. 12:1)?

- Discuss both the possibilities and the challenges of engaging in acts of resistance to policies and practices that perpetuate racial injustice.

Close discussion by spending time exploring the New Testament image of the body of Christ.

- In what ways does *body of Christ* define how we are to be in relationship with each other?
- In what ways does *body of Christ* define what happens at the Lord's Table with each other?

Chapter 4

TIME

The sabbath was made for humankind, and not humankind for the sabbath.

—Mark 2:27

THE ADVERSARIES OF JESUS, THE PHARISEES, HAD GOTTEN control of their schedule. It is no small matter to get control of one's schedule, especially in a demanding rat-race economy like ours. But actually the Pharisees had not gotten control of their schedule. To the contrary, their schedule had gotten control of them. They had only to look at the calendar to know what the particular day required of them, and what the day prohibited. This domination by the calendar is not unlike that of my mother and many other mother-housewives of her generation: "Monday is wash day, Tuesday is ironing," and so on. It is then no surprise that the Pharisees are vigilant about Sabbath day, when they sharply disapprove of the conduct of Jesus' disciples. They

53

know that what his disciples have done on the Sabbath day violates the calendar of prohibitions. They have "plucked heads of grain" to eat (Mark 2:23), and their "work" by definition violates the Sabbath.

Jesus joins issue with the defenders of the Sabbath. He defends and justifies the "violation" by the disciples. He does not say that Sabbath rules are bad or that his friends are free to do whatever they want on Sabbath. Rather he asserts that his purpose (as "Son of Man") trumps Sabbath rules. The disciples are "to act as though the kingdom of God is present."[1] And that means they are free to act and compelled to act for the sake of human welfare, in this case to deal with their own bodily hunger. On the one hand, against his adversaries Jesus radically redefines Sabbath. On the other hand, he reiterates the deepest impulse of the Sabbath command of Moses, namely, the emancipated well-being of the covenanted community. That vigorous insistence is sharply reinforced in the next textual unit, Mark 3:1–6, in which Jesus, in terse fashion, heals on the Sabbath. He restores the withered hand of the man in front of him. In the new rule of God embodied by Jesus, all times, including Sabbath time, are for the sake of human restoration.

We may take it as a truism that Sabbath is the pivotal issue concerning time in the horizon of mature materiality. Sabbath is the defining moment in all time. All six previous days of the week move toward Sabbath time. It is so for the creation as it is for the Creator (Gen. 2:1–4a). Indeed in Exodus 31:17 we are told what happened to the Creator on the seventh day, when God rested. Our translations say that God was "refreshed."

But the Hebrew word translated "refreshed" is the verbal form of the word for "self" (*nephesh*), that is, God was *re-selfed* after the depleting work of creation. So the human self is depleted or talked out of the self over six rigorous days amid the rat race of the predatory economy. The seventh day is for recovery, celebration, reordering, and affirmation of the human self. In Mark 2:23–28, Sabbath restoration occurs by *eating*. In Mark 3:1–6, it is by *healing*. Sabbath rest becomes elemental and indispensable for the well-being of the self.

Unreflective Americans want to abrogate Sabbath by endless busyness, by 24/7 electronic connection, by the practice of spectator sports, and by other preoccupations that numb the human heart and detract from the beauty of the human person. It was already like that in Pharaoh's ancient Egypt. In that regime there was no rest or relief from the incessant production requirements of Pharaoh.[2] Then, dramatically, at Mount Sinai, Moses offers ten rules for resistance to Pharaoh's ten commandments, ten guidelines for an alternative neighborly economy (Exod. 20:1–17). At the center of this new ten is Sabbath (vv. 8–11). Moses understood that resistance to and refusal of the insatiable demands of Pharaoh require attentive disciplines.

Now as then, keeping Sabbath is refusal to have one's life defined by the production and consumption demands of a commoditized economy. In the keeping of Sabbath we, like ancient Israel, attest that our lives are not defined by or answerable to the insatiability of commodity. In that ancient world, Sabbath broke the spell of production. In our world, Sabbath invites living in the new rule of God that contradicts the fatiguing world of things. Sabbath keeping is indeed acting as though Jesus is Lord of our time and has decisively trumped the rigors of our schedule!

From that discernment of Sabbath, mature materiality has radically resituated all of our times with reference to the new rule of God. Thus the psalmist can aver: "My times are in your hand" (Ps. 31:15). All my times! All our times! Not just Sabbath time but all our days. Mature materiality consists in a willing readiness to recognize that every time is a gift from God; every time is an occasion for response to the holy time-giver; every time is an opportunity to act out our glad creatureliness in ways that befit the time-giving God.

This affirmation by the psalmist occurs in a prayer in the midst of a deep crisis. The psalmist is in desperate need and has no resources. The affirmation admits that I myself do not have resources to cope with such threat. However, the statement also is a grateful recognition that "my times" are not in the hand of my adversaries; those who would do me ill do not control my times or my life. Mature materiality, then, is an acknowledgment that all days are gifts, and consequently all days are days for response and obligation. On the one hand, such awareness declares an end of *indulgent autonomy*. On the other hand, it is refusal of *demands imposed* by Pharaoh, by the Pharisees, or by the consumer economy. It is an appreciation of time as a zone of engaged freedom, freedom for human well-being, freedom for ministering to human hunger, freedom for restoration of lost human health, and freedom for glad well-being in the restorative presence of God. The psalmist can affirm:

O how abundant is your goodness
that you have laid up for those who fear you,
and accomplished for those who take refuge in you,
in the sight of everyone!
In the shelter of your presence you hide them
from human plots;
you hold them safe under your shelter
from contentious tongues.

Ps. 31:19–20

Every time is in God's hand! This means that mature materiality will know exactly what time it is, not clock time, but time in the governance of the good creator. After we confess that all times are in God's hand, we may properly differentiate some times from other times in order to know what is important and appropriate at any particular time.

It is the work of mature materiality to differentiate the times (see Matt. 16:3). For this work, we get some clarification from the "recital of the seasons" in Ecclesiastes 3:1–8. The introductory verse to this text affirms that everything has an appropriate time, that all times are in the horizon of "heaven," perhaps a side reference to the structure of creation and therefore to the creator in whose hand are all times. Sibley Towner judges that all of these pairs of times invite a moral choice except the first, concerning birth and death (v. 2), over which human persons have no discretionary power.[3] As we will see later on, in the light of scientific advance and changing cultural perspectives it is likely that even birth and death present moral choices. This recital of the seasons clearly invites attentive awareness concerning what time it is, what is appropriate to the time. It is not necessary that we consider in detail each of these time pairs in Ecclesiastes, but we may comment on several of them.

We may take the three word pairs in verses 2–3 as a set:

Plant / pluck up
Kill / heal
Break down / build up

Perhaps the three pairs are arranged in something of a chiastic order, as "plant" at the beginning and "build up" at the end are positive words that bracket two negatives, "pluck up" and "break down." The three negatives (pluck up, kill, break down) bespeak a sad and even violent ending of something, whereas the three positives (plant, heal, build up) anticipate either a new beginning or restoration of what had been damaged or lost. The three negatives witness to a reality that something must come to an end and must be relinquished.[4] There are times appropriate for *relinquishment* of what we have treasured. Conversely the positives affirm that something that was lost or nonexistent can now be initiated afresh. There are times appropriate for *receiving* that which is beyond our control or imagination.

In the book of Jeremiah, the first and third of these word pairs are frequently reiterated (1:10; 18:7–9; 24:6; 31:28; 45:4) and function as a leitmotif for the book. The negatives refer to the demise and destruction of Jerusalem, the temple, and the Davidic state of Judah. In the horizon of Jeremiah this violent ending (accomplished by the Babylonian army) is taken to be the work of YHWH. God wills *the ending* of the chosen city, chosen temple, and chosen king! Conversely, the uses of "plant" and "build" in Jeremiah concern *the inexplicable restoration* of Jerusalem and Judah and the rebuilding of the temple (by the Persians) as the will of YHWH.

When we apply this prophetic trope to the New Testament, we are able to see that "pluck up, tear down" concerns the crucifixion of Jesus, taken in Christian confession as the execution of the Messiah (see John 2:19–22). Conversely "plant and build" concerns the wondrous Easter resurrection of Jesus. Clearly Christian faith pivots around this ending and this beginning, and invites us to ponder when it is the right time to engage the reality of *Good Friday grief* and when it is the right time to engage in *Easter celebration*.

If we attend to this word pair, we may ask, as a practice of mature materiality, what now is being plucked up and torn down. It seems clear enough that the violent ideologies of race, class, gender, and white nationalism are under profound critique and assault. Conversely, we are witnessing the planting and building of a new social world of multicultural openness that attests the love of neighbor toward those who happen to be different from us. Knowing when the time is right will permit and mandate mature persons to weigh in on both *the relinquishment* of what is ending and *the welcome* of what is now emerging according to the gospel.

To these word pairs of Ecclesiastes 3 we may add the word pair in verse 7, "keep silence / speak." The prophet Amos judges that there are times to be wisely silent:

Therefore the prudent will keep silent in such a time;
for it is an evil time.

                                                    Amos 5:13

It is also the case, however, that with the current upheavals in our society there is often a pathos-filled admission, "I kept silent when I should have spoken." There is no doubt that silence out of cowardice amounts to collusion with socioeconomic arrangements that need to be protested and altered.[5] On the other hand, speaking out is a risk that must often be run, when the truth must be told. We may anticipate that those who practice mature materiality will not flinch from such times and will run the appropriate risk, not missing the fact that there is "a time to speak."

The two word pairs in verse 4 are "weep/laugh" and "mourn/dance." These word pairs are given particular nuance in the Lukan version of Jesus' Beatitudes:

Blessed are you who weep now,
for you will laugh.
. . . .
Woe to you who are laughing now,
for you will mourn and weep
                         Luke 6:21, 25

In this reading the two "times" are now and soon. If we consider only our material condition now, those who are well off might treasure the present social arrangements, find ample happiness and laughter in them, and imagine the present lasting to perpetuity. At the same time, those who are mainly left behind and left out might for good reason weep now at the lack of food, housing, or health care. According to Luke, Jesus anticipated a mighty reversal of fortunes as the kingdom of God comes. In that reversal those who laugh now will weep soon at their loss, and those who weep now will soon find happiness in their new situation (see Mic. 2:4). While the statement in Ecclesiastes seems to be morally neutral, imposing "now/soon" on the terms by Jesus creates a moral urgency to not treasure present arrangements too deeply, for such arrangements will all be lost in God's newly configured realm. Or as the psalmist has it:

> Weeping may linger for the night,
> but joy comes with the morning.
> . . . .
> You have turned my mourning into dancing;
> you have taken off my sackcloth
> and clothed me with joy.
>
> Ps. 30:5, 11

This statement is offered from those who "weep now"; they are the ones who live in a long nightmare of suffering. But not to perpetuity! Before long, matters will be different, and then will come joy. This response to that season of suffering is passionately voiced by Martin Luther King in his oration capping the march from Selma:

> "How long will justice be crucified, and truth bear it?" I come to say to you this afternoon, however difficult the moment, however frustrating the hour, it will not be long, because "truth crushed to earth will rise again." How long? Not long, because "no lie can live forever." How long? Not long, because "you

shall reap what you sow." . . . How long? Not long, because the arc of the moral universe is long, but it bends toward justice.[6]

This way of making a response appropriate to the moment must be fully in sync with God's mighty governance that can and will reverse fortunes.

To these word pairs we may add one more that is not in the book of Ecclesiastes: There is a time to go slow; there is a time to have speed.

There are times to hurry. Israel *hurried* to depart from Pharaoh's Egypt (Exod. 12:11, Deut. 16:3; but see Isa. 52:12). The shepherds *hurried* to see the wonder at Bethlehem (Luke 2:16). Zacchaeus *hurried* to dine with Jesus (Luke 19:5). The psalmist *hurried* to keep Torah (Ps. 119:60). But hurrying can also be recklessly self-destructive:

> The faithful will abound with blessings,
> but one who is in a hurry to be rich will not go
>   unpunished
>
> Prov. 28:20

As an alternative to such a rush to make a quick buck, Isaiah sees that "slow" is the proper mode for the faithful who are not propelled by greedy anxiety: "One who trusts will not panic" (Isa. 28:16).

Isaiah had already warned about the threat of military assault and cited a child appropriately named "spoil speeds, prey hastens" (Isa. 8:1). The prophet reprimands the king for his military panic and urges him to "stand firm in faith" in God. Faith is an alternative to such an anxious rush (7:9). For that reason, those who trust in God's rule do not panic and rush to self-destructive action:

> In returning and rest you will be saved;
> in quietness and in trust shall be your strength.
>
> Isa. 30:15

The prophet urges calm in the face of threat; but then in verses 16–17 he describes the mad rush to self-destruction:

> But you refused and said,
> "No! We will flee upon horses"—
> therefore you shall flee!
> and, "We will ride upon swift steeds"—
> therefore your pursuers shall be swift!
> A thousand shall flee at the threat of one,
> at the threat of five you shall flee,
> until you are left
> like a flagstaff on the top of a mountain,
>   like a signal on a hill.

The poet anticipates that his people will be devoured by anxiety.

The matter of "slow/speed" is urgent in our time. Mark C. Taylor has detailed the way in which the ideology of the market has made speed and efficiency primary virtues.[7] The cost of such a rush is immense in terms of tradition, culture, memory, and our capacity for humanness and neighborliness. Speed goes with commoditization. On the other hand, Carl Honoré has considered the quality of slowness that "challenges the cult of speed."[8] It is worth noting that the regulation of time in worldwide terms was accomplished in the service of the British navy, that is, in the service of power and control. Honoré nicely observes: "The telling time went hand in hand with telling people what to do."[9]

There is indeed a time to hurry and a time to wait. The tilt of the matter in our society is obvious. The frantic pace of overanxious 24/7 attentiveness and endless electronic connection requires that our accent in this added word pair must be on the side of slowness. Whereas *speed* is all on the side of *commoditization*, *slowness* is all on the side of *neighborliness.*

Finally we may note that the Blumhardts, Johann and Christoph, in their nineteenth-century German piety, nicely offered dialectic of "slow/speed" with their aphorism, "Make haste and wait." The art of "waiting" is urgent in mature materiality:

> Those who wait for the LORD shall renew their
>   strength,
> they shall mount up with wings like eagles,
> they shall run and not be weary,
> they shall walk and not faint.
>
> Isa. 40:31

We may now return to the initial word pair of Ecclesiastes 3:1, "be born / die." I have suggested that even this word pair entails an acute moral dimension. It is now possible (and thinkable) that we may exercise moral agency in matters of birth and death. The moral dimensions of birthing are everywhere under discussion among us. Thus I will comment on the moral dimensions concerning "a time to die." I will do so through the knowing analysis of Barbara Ehrenreich, who shows how dying is a moral issue.[10] (Ehrenreich takes a naturalistic approach to death and has no evident interest in theological considerations. Nevertheless, her analysis is compellingly instructive.) She is concerned with the zeal of our culture to extend life endlessly by medical means. The culmination of that zeal is in the onerous yearning of Silicon Valley, specifically Peter Thiel, to make immortality possible for some of the privileged. The subtitle of Ehrenreich's book *Natural Causes* ends with *Killing Ourselves to Live Longer*, which refers to the remarkable impact of medical experimentation in order to sustain the human body past its seemingly natural limit. Such an aggressive enterprise is an illusion grounded in a quite passionate rationalism that imagines that the human body can be defeated.

In the context of that seduction, Ehrenreich distances herself from such anxious medical practice, and affirms:

> Once I realized I was old enough to die, I decided that I was also old enough not to incur any more suffering, annoyance, or boredom in the pursuit of a longer life. . . . Being old enough to die is an achievement, not a defeat, and the freedom it brings is worth celebrating.[11]

Ehrenreich sees that the preoccupation with health, diet, and endless exercise is a futile attempt to maintain the isolated autonomous self in the face of death. Alternative to such an isolated self, she identifies with the verdict of Susan Sontag: "Death is unbearable unless you can get beyond the 'I.'"[12]

That is, embedment in a caring community makes it possible to face and bear death, because one sees one's self as part of a larger ongoing whole. And beyond the naturalism of Ehrenreich, our Christian confession of "the communion of saints" gives additional thickness to our capacity for freedom in the face of death. As faith affirms, this larger whole is connected to the abidingness of God. Thus in the end, mature materiality can echo the psalmist:

> So teach us to count our days
> that we may gain a wise heart.
> Ps. 90:12

The psalmist recognizes that human life is finite and limited. The psalmist does not know or want to know the exact number of allotted days but is fully honest about the existence of a limit. (Verse 10 reckons between seventy and eighty years, a limit somewhat advanced now by medical developments.) This psalm prayer recognizes that we are "dust" (v. 3); it prays for a wise heart to reckon with the reality of embodied life. That wisdom knows that our lives are bounded by "compassion" and "steadfast love" (vv. 13–14) of the God whose time is beyond our timeful reckoning (v. 4):

> The section [of the psalm] then ends with the petition for wisdom to be able to reflect on such a short life and to be able to live it fully. For the Hebrew, the heart was the center of the will or intellect, and so "a wise heart" would help people deal with the frail and brief life before them. The wisdom reflection in this petition emphasizes the trouble of life, and the plea is for the ability to deal with the reality of a frail and brief life. . . . The psalm makes it clear that human do not control life with any contrived technique or skill. Rather YHWH is the one who has created and gives life.[13]

All our times are in God's hand. Growth in mature materiality is alertness to the timefulness of every time in our life, in order that we may live it in faithful response to the Giver of all our times. Such alert responsiveness to the right moment means to yield our life back to our creator in gratitude. In such a life there will be no automatic pilot!

QUESTIONS FOR DISCUSSION

The Bible

Read aloud Exodus 20:1–11.

– To what extent do you (or do you not) experience Sabbath keeping as breaking "the spell of production" (p. 55) in our daily lives?

Read aloud Mark 2:23–3:6.

Brueggemann interprets Jesus' words and actions in this passage as making Sabbath time "the defining moment in all time" for the ultimate purpose of human restoration.

– How does this interpretation of Sabbath confirm or challenge your personal understanding and practices of Sabbath keeping?

The Book

"Mature materiality consists in a willing readiness to recognize that every time is a gift from God . . . an opportunity to act out our glad creatureliness in ways that befit the time-giving God" (p. 56).

–   Looking at our daily living, what specific actions
    affirm—or deny—that time is God's gift to us?

Brueggemann uses Ecclesiastes 3:1–8 (among other
texts) to support his claim that mature materiality
related to the concept of time involves differentiating
"some times from other times in order to know what is
important and appropriate at any particular time" (p.
57). Before discussing this section of the chapter, read
aloud the passage from Ecclesiastes.

Plant / Pluck Up; Kill/Heal;
Tear Down / Build Up

–   When have you gladly relinquished something
    you treasured? When have you received some-
    thing of a value beyond your imagining?
–   What guides our awareness of when the time
    is right to let go of something and when to wel-
    come something?

Weep/Laugh

–   How can you act in the present—especially
    toward those who "weep now"—in ways that
    anticipate the future promise of God's reversal
    of fortunes?

Silence/Speech

–   When have you felt God nudging you to respond
    to a situation, either by remaining silent or by

speaking out, when that response seemed risky but right at the moment?

Go Slow / Speed Up

- What do you lose (or what does it cost you) when speed and efficiency are the primary values that shape your daily schedule?
- When have you seen evidence of slowness being "on the side of neighborliness?" (p. 63).

Be Born / Die

- In what ways do you or can you practice the church's belief in the communion of saints?

Close by reading aloud in unison Psalm 90.

Chapter 5

PLACE

"How many of my father's hired hands have bread enough and to spare, but here I am dying of hunger! I will get up and go to my father. . . ." So he set off and went to his father.

—Luke 15:17–20

THE SON IN THE PARABLE OF THE TWO SONS WANTED OUT; he wanted to cash out his share of the family legacy and depart. His father agreed to his request. We do not know why the son wanted to leave home. Sometimes sons are like that. Perhaps he was simply venturesome and imagined an exciting life that was alternative to his settled home. Or maybe he found his father too demanding. Or maybe his entitled older brother was too much for him to bear. In any case, he left to a "distant country." There he lacked the disciplines and restraints of his home environment, and he promptly lost his inherited purse by "squandering" in "dissolute" ways. He had departed home with *u-topian* ("no-place"!) imagination, that is, he dreamed of "no place" of belonging

71

or accountability, certainly not the expectations of his home. He wound up *placeless*; he discovered that he was *homeless*. Here I will conflate "home / home place / place" so that we may consider the meaning of "home" and the deep significance of a socially located "place" as an antidote to homesickness.

His abrupt moment of awareness ("He came to himself") was materially based: he was eating pig slop! This was not his dream; this became his nightmare. He finally grasped the disconnect between *his dream* and *his bodily reality*. He could no longer permit his imagined freedom to override the truth of his hungry body. In that moment of acute self-awareness he got in touch with his body and now could imagine what it would be like to resituate his *body* in the midst of his *home place*, in the presence of his father and his brother. Robert Wuthnow nicely characterizes "home":

> Social scientists conceptualize homes as places in which we routinely interact with people we know and care about, places in which we conduct the most routine activities of our everyday lives and in which we feel or aspire to feel safe. Homes are places of familiarity, memory, ambience, and habit and for this reason are the spaces we can take for granted much of the time and in which we can be comfortable.[1]

The first draw for the son was his knowledge that at home there was bread to spare (v. 17). Like his actions, Jesus' stories characteristically witness to abundance! The father was a reliable provider. In his imagination, however, the son reached beyond bread to his father because his home place was defined by his father. He remembered, moreover, that his father had filled his home place with uncompromising expectations. Thus "I have sinned." He has, he recognized, merited the disapproval and rejection of his father, for his imagined *u-topian* ("no-place"!) life has violated all of the expectations of his home place and his father.

The first wonder of the story is that the son went home. He had discovered that without that home place, its resources, and its expectations, his life was unbearably diminished. Mature materiality is invited to reflect on what it means to belong to a home place with all of its expectations, requirements, demands, and gifts. Such reflection may also lead to fresh awareness of the cost of being without such a place, away from home. The second wonder of the story is that he was, much to his surprise, welcomed home.

The critical reflection of mature materiality concerning place (home place) might begin with a pondering of *homelessness*. Taken in largest scope, Martin Buber has written of the reality of homelessness in the modern world:

> I distinguish between epochs of habitation and epochs of homelessness. In the former, man lives in the world as in a house, as in a home. In the latter, man lives in the world as in an open field and at times does not even have four pegs with which to set up a tent.[2]

Buber contrasts modern "homelessness" with the "habitation" made possible and assumed in the Middle Ages for European Christians who lived under a "sacred canopy" of stability. The new homelessness is the result of the modern scientific Copernican revolution that caused human persons to lose their place in the cosmos:

> All the walls of the house were in fact already crumbling beneath the blows of Copernicus, the unlimited was pressing in from every side, and man was standing in a universe which in actual fact could no longer be experienced as a house. . . . The Copernican concept only fulfilled what the human soul had vaguely felt in the hours when the house of universal space . . . seemed too cramped, and it dared to beat on its walls to see if a window could not be thrown out into the world beyond.[3]

Micheal O'Siadhail, to the contrary, takes Copernicus to be a venturesome emancipator who stood over against the church:

> By stealth Copernicus has taken root
> when after sixty years of silence Rome
> joins in to forbid this teaching of the Sun.
> …
> our place between devils and the angels,
> our Earth as centre of God's universe
> all threatened by such a revolution
> that could unhinge the doors of our belief.[4]

Even his affirmative vote, however, witnesses belief "unhinge" with an open question about God and man:

> A question rattles in an empty can:
> how here could man find God or God find man?

The son in the parable did not ponder the cosmic question of Buber or the cosmic wonder of O'Siadhail. He only noticed the material void in his life, and he could still remember the rooted resources of his father

and his home place. We may, however, draw the crisis of his *u-topia* ("no-place"!) closer than Buber's cosmic dismay by considering the homelessness produced
by contemporary technology that generates "virtual
reality" but no social reality that has staying power.
Already in 1974, long before the internet, Peter Berger,
Bridgette Berger, and Hansfried Kellner wrote *The
Homeless Mind: Modernization and Consciousness*.[5] That
new reality of which Berger writes can be viewed as
a matter of emancipation from old tradition that was
often viewed as a restraint that felt like shackles. Thus
modernity took as its great work, with its pursuit of
speed, efficiency, and replaceable parts, the rejection
of tradition that must make way for the new. Such
eager emancipation left the individual isolated in freedom but without any community that provided either
resources or restraints. Thus the son, in the parable, in
a far country has no companions of any kind. He is
alone, abandoned in his lack of resources. He is a hired
hand without the protection of a trade union; he is left
desolate and desperate. The social reality of abandonment that he experienced is replicated in the "homelessness" of contemporary technology with its capacity
to radically displace.

Buber's philosophical reflection and Berger's riff on
technology are given acute specificity and contempora-
neity by the compelling analysis of Shoshana Zuboff
in *The Age of Surveillance Capitalism*.[6] Zuboff traces the
aggressive way in which the great research engines, specifically Google and Facebook, have intruded into the
most intimate and personal dimensions of our experience. Indeed our "experience" has been transposed into

marketable "behavior," so that Google and Facebook sell data about our experience to marketers in a way that contributes to the ruthless, uncaring commoditization of our lives. She describes our new social reality as one of "exile" in which we experience a loss of a capacity for privacy and intimacy. We are left, she notes, with an unbearable yearning:

> [It is] homesickness and longing of separation from the homeland [common] among emigrants across the centuries. Now the disruptions of the twenty-first century have turned these exquisite anxieties and longings of dislocation into a universal story that engulfs each one of us.[7]

We are left with what she characterizes as a "Requiem for a Home."

Mature materiality will do the hard work of making a connection between "the homeless mind" and the "homeless body," so that when we speak of homelessness—loss of place—we will have both in purview. A connection is made by Craig Fuller, who writes of his "bodily homelessness" in Seattle, the home of the great technological engines Microsoft and Amazon. Under the title "The Homeless Industrial Complex Problem," Fuller describes his own desperate homelessness in his city that is at the head of technological domination but that cannot muster resources to provide houses for those without resources.[8] We may conclude that those with *homeless minds* (generated by the new intrusive technologies) are not likely to notice those with *homeless bodies* (of the left out and left behind who live in economic isolation).

This linkage may lead mature materiality to wonder how it is that we not only live in an economy that is *occupied by homeless persons*; we live in an economy that is busy *producing homeless persons*. The capacity to produce homeless persons is deeply enmeshed in a privatized, greedy economy of low wages, predatory loan arrangements, and regressive tax policy. It is easy enough, moreover, to imagine that much of our current homelessness is a residue of slavery in which a population of laborers ended a lifetime of work with no resources.[9] So it is with us now with many workers who are not officially slaves but who end a lifetime of work without resources. That systemic production of homeless persons is a direct result of "technological homelessness" whereby the successful in the technological enterprise to some great extent have no interest in, capacity to notice, or willingness to support and pay for a viable social network for those in need of housing. The current inability to deal with student indebtedness is only a recent example of the indifference of the predatory economy to the requirements of the less privileged for a viable life support.

Berger used the word "consciousness" in his subtitle. That term refers to the power of technology to induct into an alternative way of knowing and living.[10] But "consciousness" is also the right word for what happened to the son in the parable: "He came to himself." He became conscious of his true situation of abandonment and hunger. The consciousness of which Berger writes, however, is very different. It contradicts mature materiality because it is detached from the bodily, the historical, and the social.

The son found a resolution to his abandonment. He went back home to his rightful place. He resubmitted to the reality of that place, to its requirements, to its expectations, to the expectations of his father, to the irksome presence of his brother, to a place infused with abundance and rootage, the very abundance and rootage from which he had fled. In order to start that return journey, however, he had to acknowledge his hunger; he had to abandon his *u-topian* ("no-place!") fantasy of being unfettered by his rootage. He had to recognize that his anticipation for a far country was in fact a lethal illusion. Until he came to that "consciousness," he could not make a move back to a place of human viability.

The wonder for him, of course, is that when he got home, he was welcomed. That was not what he had expected, because he had become inured to the callous indifference of the far country that never welcomed anyone and that made every relationship transactional. It turned out that his home and his *homecoming* radically contradicted his experience in the far country of *homelessness of mind and body.*

The Bible knows about the crisis of homelessness and expects that adherents to covenant will resist such predatory behavior. On the one hand, the remarkable mandate of Isaiah intends to counter homelessness by home making:

Is not this the fast that I choose:
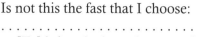
    [To] bring the homeless poor into your house;
when you see the naked, to cover them,
and not to hide yourself from your own kin?

Isa. 58:6–7

The Hebrew word translated "kin" means "flesh," the extreme articulation of solidarity. Lent, when this text from Isaiah is usually read in church, is a wondrous time to consider faithful effective strategies to respond to homeless persons. The covenantal response to homelessness is responsible solidarity that mobilizes resources sufficient for home making. In addition to such charitable investments, Zuboff urges resistance to and disruption of the uncontested force of the dominant research engines. She issues the imperative "be the friction," and concludes:

> The Berlin Wall fell for many reasons, but above all it was because the people of East Berlin said, "No more!" We too can be the authors of many "great and beautiful" new facts that reclaim the digital future as humanity's home. No more! Let this be *our* declaration.[11]

On the other hand, the covenantal tradition is aware that the predatory economy is busy "making homeless," by the ways in which the powerful prey on the vulnerable. The classic case is the narrative of Naboth's vineyard (1 Kgs. 21), in which the power of the crown preys upon a vulnerable peasant.[12] The covenantal tradition is at pains to preclude such predatory action undertaken by smart lawyers, aggressive real estate agents, or the exercise of eminent domain. The code language in Scripture concerns "moving boundary markers" whereby property is legally seized from those who cannot defend themselves and thereby wind up homeless:[13]

You must not move your *neighbor's* boundary marker,
set up by former generations, on the property that will
be allotted to you in the land that the LORD your God
is giving you to possess. (Deut. 19:14; italics added;
see Prov. 22:28)

Here it is the property of a "neighbor," the neighbor who is exactly in purview in the final of the Ten
Commandments:

You shall not covet your *neighbor's* house; you shall
not covet your *neighbor's* wife, or male or female slave,
or ox, or donkey, or anything that belongs to your
neighbor. (Exod. 20:17; italics added)

In Proverbs 23:10–11, the matter is more acute, for it
concerns "orphans" who lack a patriarchal defender:

Do not remove an ancient landmark
or encroach on the fields of *orphans*,
for their redeemer is strong;
he will plead their cause against you.
               Prov. 23:10–11; italics added;
                    see 15:25 on the boundary
                         marker of a widow

These are provisions designed to protect vulnerable
people from becoming displaced and homeless. A covenantal community (like the ones to which mature
materiality pertains) aims to refuse and resist the
u-topian ("no-place!") displacement of replaceable
parts, replaceable persons, and replaceable places.

Mature materiality, like that of the son in the parable,
knows that a faithful life requires participation in, attentiveness to, and loyalty to a place. The son came to know
this; upon his return he finds his rightful place defined

by adequate food, festive welcome, and a gracious safe-making father. Embrace of such a life-giving place presents us with two generative questions about place.

First, *where am I supposed to be?* To ask this question is already to acknowledge that there is a "right place" to be that should not be confused with the bright lights of a "far country" of *u-topia* ("no-place!") that is anti-human. A vacation in *u-topia* may be in order but, as the son discovered, it cannot become one's "continuing city" (Heb. 11:14; NRSV "homeland"). For good reason it is high praise to say of someone, "He never forgot where he came from." Everyone comes from somewhere. Everyone comes from a particular place with its particular hope and particular resources and particular social protocols and particular foods. These particulars may be amended and critiqued, but they cannot be safely scuttled in a wholesale way for the sake of rootless imagination. Thus the "right place" to be is a place that is infused with particulars that impose costs, give gifts, and offer rootage. We are not meant to be and finally cannot be rootless, placeless occupants of "nowhere"; finally we must be obligated, contributing partners in a time and place.

The vow of "stability" taken by some monks is instructive. That vow means to spend one's life invested "on location" without the illusion that elsewhere, any elsewhere, would be preferable. Thus a "place" is an actual human venue in which one puts down one's buckets in durable ways. For many persons the liturgy of a particular religious community lends staying power to a place. This is true in Christian liturgy, and no less true in other traditions as well.

Second, we may ask about our right place, *how is it that I should inhabit that particular place of home?* Well, NOT as *user, consumer, possessor, exploiter,* or *predator.* These are models of occupation that are appropriate for a commoditized society in which those with "homeless minds" are unable to care about those with "homeless bodies." Mature materiality rejects and refuses all such convenient modes of habitation that are marked by indifference, apathy, fatigue, or selfishness. The intention of mature materiality is to identify and enact more appropriate forms of habitation. Here are four markers for such responsible habitation:

1. Mature habitation of one's right place is as an *heir.* The son in the parable was an heir, but he had forgotten that as an heir he not only owned the land but the land owned him. He belonged to the land. When he forgot his role as an heir, he could depart into a far country. When he returned to his father, however, he reentered his legacy and knew, from that moment, that he belonged to the land and it was his place of being and belonging.

In his narrative, Naboth is an example of a responsible heir (1 Kgs. 21). The royal power couple, Ahab and Jezebel, regard Naboth's vineyard as a fungible piece of property for buying and selling. They think about every place through the lens of commodity. Naboth, however, knows better. He knows that his vineyard property is not fungible. It cannot be "transacted" but, as he asserts, it is his "ancestral inheritance" (v. 3). It has always been the home of his family. It is where he belongs. He must work and protect the vineyard because he belongs to it. This narrative is a

stark example of two modes of habitation that clash
(see Buber). Here, in this narrative as almost always,
the force of *commoditization* seems to have the upper
hand, a fact that makes habitation as *inheritance* difficult. The narrative attests, however, that the God who
gives a livable place is fully on the side of such habitation that can so readily be overturned by usurpation.
Wendell Berry has educated us all about the land as
inheritance that cannot be traded as fungible property.[14] Mature materiality requires a full commitment
to such regard for one's right place and equal regard
for the right place of the neighbor, including the vulnerable neighbor. In our society it is the aggression of
gentrification that most readily puts vulnerable inheritance at risk.[15]

2. The right way to inhabit one's right place is as
neighbor. The role of neighbor pertains not only to
next-door folk with whom we may feel comfortable.
It means also to recognize all the inhabitants of the
community as companions in a common enterprise.
It means to acknowledge gladly that they are entitled
to respect, safety, and viability that are guaranteed
by common concern and common investment. In a
commoditized economy, there are no neighbors with
whom we can make common cause. There are only
isolated individuals who live private lives and who
are at bottom rivals and competitors for scarce goods.
Neighborliness refuses every part of that formulation:
not isolated, not rivals, not competitors, and not scarce
goods. The neighborhood depends on an expectation
and practice of generosity and a readiness to share
what one has for the sake of the common good. Such

generosity pertains not only to those whom we like and with whom we feel comfortable. Such sharing, moreover, consists not only in face-to-face generosity, but in sustainable transformative charity and, beyond that, in acceptance of taxation that is appropriate to the needs of the neighborhood.

The mandate to "love your neighbor" (Lev. 19:18; Mark 12:31) is defining for mature materiality. This commandment, Paul declares, is "the whole law [Torah] summed up" (Gal. 5:14). The biblical tradition, moreover, continues to expand the scope of "neighbor" until it includes all the vulnerable, for whom "widow, orphan, and immigrant" are representative persons.

3. Mature materiality requires that we inhabit our right place as *partners with the place*. Thus rather than the place belonging to the "owner," in partnership the place and the owner belong to each other and are cast together in a long-range destiny. It follows that the owner is assigned to a purpose not of maximizing production, but rather of enhancing the well-being of the home place. Wendell Berry writes of "kindly use" of the land that depends upon intimate knowledge of the terrain of the property.[16] The purpose of such "kindly use" is the prospect of durability in the right place, an assumption that coming generations may inhabit this right place. Thus the owner of the right place is not the final occupant but in fact belongs to a long chain of those who have inhabited and who will inhabit in time to come.

4. Mature materiality requires that one be alert to one's role as *citizen*, that is, having active responsibility

for the public good. This responsibility evokes participation in the political life of the community and
a readiness to engage with other neighbors in the
demanding work that submits private interests to the
public good.

I should add a note about the right place being variously rural or urban.[17] It is an easier case to make one's
practice of habitation as *heir, neighbor, partner,* and *citizen* in a rural community where institutions are more
accessible, where the population is more likely to be
homogeneous, and where face-to-face interactions are
more readily available. Such a portrayal of rural habitation may be tempted to romanticism. But to refuse
romanticism about rural life (as Wendell Berry refuses)
one must recognize that rural life is not on offer for
everyone. Many persons will, for a variety of reasons,
be urban dwellers. In densely occupied urban habitats,
the same call to be *heir, neighbor, partner,* and *citizen* is
sounded. Only there it is more complex and in some
ways more demanding. But these same markers for
the right place pertain, even if on a different scale. In
urban settings one can more feel detached from such a
summons. For that reason the insistence of the urban
church on right habitation is all the more important.
The church community can vouch for a narrative of
responsible habitation and be a body of companions
engaged in good work for the "right place."

In both urban and rural settings there will be
many who are "homeless" and lack a right place. For
some it will be a *homeless mind,* a life of focused on
virtual reality rather than on the real neighborhood.
For many others it will be *homeless bodies* that are

rendered destitute by a predatory economy that willfully "leaves behind." In the face of such dual "homelessness," mature materiality is to be engaged in home making. As we do so, the best affirmation is this most direct one:

> 'Tis the gift to be simple,
> 'Tis the gift to be free,
> 'Tis the gift to come down where we ought to be.[18]

The operational word is "gift."[19] Being in the right place is a gift, not an achievement. If it were an achievement, one could imagine one is entitled and owes no one anything. If, however, a right place is a gift, then the appropriate response is gratitude, a practice that sends us passionately back into the neighborhood in a way that notices the *homeless* (*homeless minds, homeless bodies*), and that does *home making* after the manner of the home-making God:

> For the LORD your God is God of gods and Lord of lords, the great God, mighty and awesome, who is not partial and takes no bribe, who executes justice for the orphan and the widow, and who loves the strangers, providing them food and clothing. You shall also love the stranger, for you were strangers in the land of Egypt. (Deut. 10:17–19)

I will end with the wise counsel of David Brooks:

> We are bound together by our affection for our place. . . . Out-radicalize the left and the right by offering a different system of power, a system in which power is wielded by neighbors, who know their local context and trust one another.[20]

QUESTIONS FOR DISCUSSION

The Bible

Brueggemann weaves two primary biblical texts throughout his comments in this chapter: Luke 15:11–32 (parable of the Two Sons) and 1 Kings 21:1–16 (Naboth's vineyard). Consider reading both at the start of the group's discussion, inviting participants to be mindful of when they can inform their responses to the material in the chapter.

The Book

Consider beginning with the ending: recall the chapter's closing quote from David Brooks: "We are bound together by our affection for our place" (p. 86).

- What in your experience makes that statement ring true? Or false?

Key points in Jesus' parable of the Two Sons are (1) the prodigal son *went* home, and (2) he was *welcomed* home.

- What does it mean to belong to a home place?
- What are the costs of being away from a home place?

In citing the writings of Zuboff (pp. 75–79), Brueggemann calls attention to her description of our present social reality as a kind of exile, "in which we experience a loss of capacity for privacy and intimacy."

- To what extent do you feel as though you live in exile? What other images might better convey your experience?

Brueggemann appeals to Isaiah 58 to call for "home making" to be the proper response of mature faith to the homelessness of mind and body in our society.

- Where do you see evidence that we live in an economy that is both occupied by and produces homeless persons?
- What attitudes, actions, and resources are needed for us to counter homelessness with home making?

Just as the son in Jesus' parable found his rightful place when he returned home, Brueggemann claims that "a faithful life requires participation in, attentiveness to, and loyalty to a place" (p. 80). Two questions follow:

- Where are you supposed to be? What is the place you are rooted in and contribute to?
- How should you inhabit your "right" place to be?

The question about how we should inhabit our home places invites further discussion around what Brueggemann identifies as five "models of occupation" and "four markers of responsible habitation" (pp. 82–85).

- How do you inhabit your home place as *user, consumer, possessor, exploiter, predator*?
- How do you inhabit your home place as *heir, neighbor, partner, citizen*?

Close your discussion by reciting together the familiar Shaker hymn lyric on page 86.

CONCLUSION

The gifts he gave were that some would be apostles, some prophets,
some evangelists, some pastors and teachers, to equip the saints for
the work of ministry, for building up the body of Christ, until all of
us come to the unity of the faith and of the knowledge of the Son
of God, to maturity, to the measure of the full stature of Christ. We
must no longer be children.

—Ephesians 4:11–14

A STUDY OF CHRISTIAN MATERIALITY EXHIBITS A CONVER-
gence of two realities. On the one hand, the Bible itself
is preoccupied, as I have shown, with matters material. It
is a misreading of the Bible to imagine otherwise. On the
other hand, our lives are preoccupied with matters material that claim most of our energy and imagination and
that evoke for us, variously, hope and anxiety. To imagine
otherwise about our lives is an illusion. The convergence
of *the materiality of our lives* and *the materiality of the Bible*
commends us to think honestly, critically, and faithfully
about the material dimensions of our lives according to
the purposes and promises of the God of the gospel.

We can readily identify five key terms of covenantal
fidelity that fully characterize the way in which we may

love God and love neighbor. God's self-giving vow to God's covenantal partner, Israel, goes like this:

> I will take you for my wife forever; I will take you for my wife in *righteousness* and in *justice*, in *steadfast love*, and in *mercy*. I will take you for my wife in *faithfulness*; and you shall know the LORD. (Hos. 2:19–20; italics added)

This vow voiced by God, albeit in deeply patriarchal terms, pivots on five words. In this text these five terms—*righteousness, justice, steadfast love, mercy*, and *faithfulness*—indicate God's way with us. But the same terms pertain when we respond to God. We are to practice *justice, righteousness, steadfast love, mercy*, and *faithfulness* as an act of fidelity toward God. When we consider this as a way of loving neighbor, however, it is clear that we show this way of fidelity through the material dimensions of our life together. Thus mature materiality is the practice of *justice, righteousness, steadfast love, mercy,* and *faithfulness* with the neighbor with reference to such matters as *money, food, bodily health, time,* and *place.*

In order for this practice to be durable intentionally, honestly, and knowingly, it is essential that we develop disciplines and practices that will sustain this way of being in a culture that is elementally adverse to such a practice. Most of us are, in fact, not unlike the "infants" in Hebrews 5 who are not yet "trained by practice" for the mature materiality that is required for good neighborliness. Thus the intent of this study is to point to the urgency of faithful disciplines and practices that will let mature materiality be central to our faithfulness.

If we are to embrace such disciplines and practices, then almost all of us require guidance and support. As a result I propose that church leaders, specifically pastors, might think of themselves as "directors of materiality." I have a hope that we may consider this role as a parallel to the long-standing practice of "spiritual direction" that helps so many of us to embrace the skills, disciplines, and sensibility for our spiritual life. We also require such direction for our faithful materiality. If we heed the summons of the Epistle to the Ephesians to "equip the saints" for "maturity to the measure of the full stature of Christ," it follows that it is the work of ministry to evoke the skills and faculties for discernment and action in the arena of materiality. If and when pastors willingly take on the role of directors of materiality, in turn curricular studies may emerge that focus on materiality. In the long run I anticipate that theological faculties that educate clergy will offer programmatic study for directors of materiality.

This present study in no way denigrates or undercuts an ancient accent on spirituality. I have no doubt, moreover, that from an honest gospel-focused attentiveness to mature materiality, a fresh and vibrant spirituality will emerge. We are led to see that a mature, obedient materiality is indeed a glad response to the creator God who has come bodied in Jesus of Nazareth. Thus we may address the dualism that has for much too long vexed the modern church.

We know of the affirmation of 1 John 4:20: "Those who do not love a brother or sister whom they have seen, cannot love God whom they have not seen." We are commended to love both God and neighbor. We dare to judge that these two loves are in truth one love. The way we love God is to love neighbors in their full materiality. In commenting on the good king Josiah, Jeremiah can aver:

> Did not your father [King Josiah] eat and drink
> and do justice and righteousness?
> Then it was well with him.
> He judged the cause of the poor and needy;
> then it was well.
> Is not this to know me?
> says the LORD.
>
> Jer. 22:15–16

The prophet does not say that if we know God, then we will do justice for the needy. Nor does the prophet say that if we do justice for the needy, then we will know God. Rather than either of these, he asserts that love of neighbor (brother, sister) is itself the way we know God. This is to know God! José Miranda says of this remarkable prophetic claim: "Yahweh is known only in the human act of achieving justice and compassion for the neighbor."[1]

Such justice and compassion will well up in and through mature materiality. This is now an urgent gospel mandate in a culture that is at work dismissing the claim of the neighbor. It is crucial that the church not collude with that predatory dismissal of the neighbor. Mature materiality is a venture and a passion that refuses the predation of a commoditized society. Mature materiality requires solid food beyond milk on offer for babies.

NOTES

Introduction

1. Peter Brown, *Through the Eye of a Needle: Wealth, the Fall of Rome, and the Making of Christianity in the West, 350–550 AD* (Princeton, NJ: Princeton University Press, 2012).
2. Brown, 517.
3. William Barclay, quoted by Edgar McKnight in *Hebrews–James*, Smyth & Helwys Bible Commentary (Macon, GA: Smyth & Helwys, 2004), 131.

Chapter 1: Money

1. See Jacques Ellul, *Money and Power* (Downers Grove, IL: InterVarsity Press, 1984).
2. Roland Boer, *The Sacred Economy of Ancient Israel* (Louisville, KY: Westminster John Knox Press, 2015), 202–3.
3. Boer, 202–3.

4. Wendell Berry, *The Art of Loading Brush: New Agrarian Writings* (Berkeley, CA: Counterpoint, 2017), 117.

5. Berry, 103.

6. Wendell Berry, *The World-Ending Fire: The Essential Wendell Berry* (Berkeley, CA: Counterpoint, 2017), 232.

7. Berry, 259.

8. Berry, 263.

9. On the Lord's Prayer and its linkage to the year of Jubilee, see Douglas Oakman, *Jesus, Debt, and the Lord's Prayer: First-Century Debt and Jesus' Intent* (Eugene, OR: Cascade Books, 2014), and Sharon Ringe, *Jesus, Liberation, and the Biblical Jubilee: Images for Ethics and Christology*, Overtures to Biblical Theology 19 (Philadelphia: Fortress Press, 1985). More broadly on debt and debt forgiveness, see David Graeber, *Debt: The First 5,000 Years* (New York: Melville House, 2011). Graeber has no noticeable interest in theology or ethics; nevertheless his book ends with an affirmation that the only viable way to handle the international debt crisis is by way of a Jubilee. Mature materiality has an opportunity to rethink economics through the lens of debt cancellation and apart from debt-producing market ideology.

10. Fred Dickey, "Arianna Huffington Is a Brilliant, Captivating, Wickedly Funny Enemy of the Establishment. She Also May Be a World-Class Opportunist," *Los Angeles Times*, July 30, 2000, https://www.latimes.com/archives/la-xpm-2000-jul-30-tm-61409-story.html.

Chapter 2: Food

1. James C. Scott, *Against the Grain: A Deep History of the Earliest States* (New Haven, CT: Yale University Press, 2017), explores the way in which states, even the earliest states, have worked to achieve a monopoly on grain as a mode of controlling wealth. The practice of Pharaoh in Gen. 47:13–26 illustrates the administrative power that Scott articulates. Grain became a vehicle for monopolistic power because it can be produced on a predictable schedule and be stored for a long time, and therefore can be administered according to the policies of the monopolizing power. The insatiable man

in the parable of Jesus reflects this eagerness for excessive grain storage.

2. My friend Peter Block has called my attention to the way in which TV ads work. The ad promises that the purchase of the product will make the viewer safe, healthy, or happy. The necessary assumption that remains tacit is that the consumer has been not safe, not healthy, or not happy, because otherwise there would be no need for the product. Thus such marketing can never affirm present well-being but can only promise future well-being assured by the product.

3. Wendell Berry, *Jayber Crow: A Novel* (Washington, DC: Counterpoint, 2000), 181.

4. Wendell Berry, *The World-Ending Fire: The Essential Wendell Berry* (Berkeley, CA: Counterpoint, 2017), 149.

5. Ellen F. Davis, *Scripture, Culture, and Agriculture: An Agrarian Reading of the Bible* (Cambridge: Cambridge University Press, 2009), 103–4.

6. See Brooks Harrington, *No Mercy, No Justice: The Dominant Narrative of America versus the Counter-Narrative of Jesus' Parables* (Eugene, OR: Cascade Books, 2019), 184–98.

7. From Brooks Harrington, *No Mercy, No Justice: The Dominant Narrative of America versus the Counter-Narrative of Jesus' Parables* (Eugene: Cascade Books, 2019).

8. Cameron Whybrow, *The Bible, Baconianism, and Mastery over Nature: The Old Testament and Its Modern Misreading* (New York: Peter Lang, 1991), provides a reliable guide to the way in which the assumptions of modernity (with particular reference to Francis Bacon) have regarded nature as an object to be exploited for human satisfaction. The notion of partnership with creation constitutes a frontal contradiction to that modernist assumption.

9. Matthias Claudius, "We Plow the Fields and Scatter," *Prayer Book and Hymnal according to the Use of the Episcopal Church* (New York: Church Publishing, 1986), 291. I am surprised to discover that this hymn has been omitted from the most recent hymnals of the United Church of Christ, the United Methodist Church, and the Presbyterian Church (U.S.A.), perhaps in the mistaken assumption that we have

"advanced" beyond such intimate contact with the soil and God's gift of food production. Alas!

Chapter 3: The Body

1. Samuel John Stone, "The Church's One Foundation," *Glory to God* (Louisville, KY: Westminster John Knox Press, 2013), 321.

2. The dangers of such patriarchal imagery must be fully taken into account, as is done by Renita J. Weems, *Battered Love: Marriage, Sex, and Violence in the Hebrew Prophets*, Overtures to Biblical Theology (Minneapolis: Fortress Press, 1995).

3. The radicality of the imagery is indicated by the use the prophet Jeremiah makes of the old Torah tradition. In Deut. 24:1–4 the Torah prohibits the return of a compromised wife to her husband, thus protecting patriarchal honor. But in Jer. 3:1–4:4, God willingly violates that law for the sake of a restored relationship. See Michael Fishbane, *Biblical Interpretation in Ancient Israel* (Oxford: Clarendon Press, 1985), 307–12.

4. Nadia Bolz-Weber, *Shameless: A Sexual Reformation* (New York: Convergent, 2019).

5. The disastrous decision by the global United Methodist Church in February 2019 to continue to reject same-sex marriage and gay clergy is a glaring case in which preoccupation with body parts has trumped matters of covenantal fidelity, much to the shame of the body of Christ. Perfect fear drives out love (cf. 1 John 4:18)!

6. Roy Schaeffer, *Retelling a Life: Narration and Dialogue in Psychoanalysis* (New York: Basic Books, 1992), 94–95, articulates the dynamic, dialogic quality of sexual interaction in his recognition that the whole person in a sexual relation must be, variously, both "agent" and "milieu."

7. A biblical understanding of the "body" as the whole person is expressed in the Hebrew term *nephesh*, which we variously translate as "soul" or "self." On that dynamism, see Hans Walter Wolff, *Anthropology of the Old Testament* (Mifflintown, PA: Sigler Press, 1974), 76–79.

8. N. T. Wright, "The Letter to the Romans," in *The New Interpreter's Bible* (Nashville: Abingdon Press, 2002), 10:705.

9. See Philip Carrington, *The Primitive Christian Catechism: A Study in the Epistles* (Cambridge: Cambridge University Press, 1940).

10. Brigitte Kahl, *Galatians Re-Imagined: Reading with the Eyes of the Vanquished* (Minneapolis: Fortress Press, 2010), 270 and passim, shows how these two catalogs reflect the force of the Roman Empire and the new regime of the gospel. They are not simply moral qualities but practices embedded in competing ideological claims.

11. Ta-Nehisi Coates, *Between the World and Me* (New York: Spiegel & Grau, 2015), 33.

12. Coates, 50.

13. Coates, 116.

14. Coates, 110–11.

15. Coates, 101. Sven Beckert, *Empire of Cotton: A Global History* (New York: Alfred A. Knopf, 2014), shows how the culture of cotton production everywhere through history is infused with brutality and violence. The history of cotton in the United States is a prime example.

16. See Michelle Alexander, *The New Jim Crow: Mass Incarceration in the Age of Colorblindness* (New York: New Press, 2010), and Carol Anderson, *White Rage: The Unspoken Truth of Our Racial Divide* (New York: Bloomsbury, 2016).

17. See John Fawcett, "Blest Be the Tie That Binds," *Glory to God*, 306; see also my commentary on the hymn, Walter Brueggemann, *A Glad Obedience: Why and What We Sing* (Louisville, KY: Westminster John Knox Press, 2019), 65–70.

18. Dietrich Bonhoeffer, *The Cost of Discipleship* (New York: Macmillan, 1948), 183.

19. Andrea Bieler and Louise Schottroff, *The Eucharist: Bodies, Bread, & Resurrection* (Minneapolis: Fortress Press, 2007), 41.

20. Bieler and Schottroff, 84–85.

21. See R. Alan Streett, *Subversive Meals: An Analysis of the Lord's Supper under Roman Domination during the First Century* (Eugene, OR: Pickwick Press, 2013). In the same connection, see also R. Alan Streett, *Caesar and the Sacrament:*

Baptism; A Rite of Resistance (Eugene, OR: Cascade Books, 2018).

22. See William T. Cavanaugh, *Torture and Eucharist: Theology, Politics, and the Body of Christ* (Oxford: Blackwell, 1998).

Chapter 4: Time

1. Pheme Perkins, "The Gospel of Mark," in *The New Interpreter's Bible* (Nashville: Abingdon Press, 1991), 8:557.

2. It is easy enough to identify Pharaoh's "ten commandments" in Exodus 5 that prescribe endless productive performance and refuse any Sabbath rest:

> 1. "Why are you taking the people away from their work? Get to your labors!" (v. 4).
> 2. "You shall no longer give the people straw to make bricks, as before; let them go and gather straw for themselves" (v. 7).
> 3. "You shall require of them the same quantity of bricks as they made previously; do not diminish it, for they are lazy" (v. 8).
> 4. "Let heavier work be laid on them; then they will labor at it and pay no attention to deceptive words" (v. 9).
> 5. "Go and get straw yourselves, wherever you can find it; but your work will not be lessened in the least" (v. 11).
> 6. "Complete your work, the same daily assignment as when you were given straw" (v. 13).
> 7. "Why did you not finish the required quantity of bricks yesterday and today, as you did before?" (v. 14).
> 8. "You are lazy, lazy; that is why you say, 'Let us go and sacrifice to the LORD'" (v. 17).
> 9. "Go now, and work; for no straw shall be given you, but you shall still deliver the same number of bricks" (v.18).

10. "You shall not lessen your daily number of bricks" (v. 19).

See Walter Brueggemann, *Sabbath as Resistance: Saying No to a Culture of Now* (Louisville, KY: Westminster John Knox Press, 2014).

3. W. Sibley Towner, "The Book of Ecclesiastes," in *The New Interpreter's Bible* (Nashville: Abingdon Press, 1997), 5:305.

4. See Walter Brueggemann, *Tenacious Solidarity: Biblical Provocations on Race, Religion, Climate and the Economy* (Minneapolis: Fortress Press, 2018), 109–17, 175–96.

5. See Walter Brueggemann, *Interrupting Silence: God's Command to Speak Out; A Bible Study for Adults* (Louisville, KY: Westminster John Knox Press, 2018).

6. Martin Luther King Jr., "Our God Is Marching On!," Montgomery, AL, March 25, 1965, Martin Luther King, Jr. Research and Education Institute, https://kinginstitute.stanford.edu/our-god-marching.

7. Mark Taylor, *Speed Limits: Where Time Went and Why We Have So Little Left* (New Haven, CT: Yale University Press, 2014).

8. Carl Honoré, *In Praise of Slowness: Challenging the Cult of Speed* (New York: HarperCollins, 2004). See Walter Brueggemann, *Ice Axes for Frozen Seas: A Biblical Theology of Provocation*, ed. Davis Hankins (Waco, TX: Baylor University Press, 2014), 351–74.

9. Honoré, *In Praise of Slowness*, 22.

10. Barbara Ehrenreich, *Natural Causes: An Epidemic of Wellness, the Certainty of Dying, and Killing Ourselves to Live Longer* (New York: Twelve, 2018).

11. Ehrenreich, 3, 13.

12. Ehrenreich, 203. Ehrenreich notes that Sontag's son reports that in the end Sontag was unable to live out her own dictum. That of course does not keep her dictum from being true.

13. Walter Brueggemann and William H. Bellinger Jr., *Psalms*, New Cambridge Bible Commentary (Cambridge: Cambridge University Press, 2014), 392–93.

Chapter 5: Place

1. Robert Wuthnow, *The Left Behind: Decline and Rage in Rural America* (Princeton, NJ: Princeton University Press, 2018), 13. Shoshana Zuboff, *The Age of Surveillance Capitalism: The Fight for a Human Future at the New Frontier of Power* (New York: Public Affairs, 2019), 476, quotes Gaston Bachelard:

> The house shelters daydreaming, the house protects the dreamer, the house allows one to dream in peace. . . . The house is one of the greatest powers of integration for the thoughts, memories, and dreams of mankind. . . . It is body and soul. It is the human being's first world. Before he is "cast into the world," . . . man is laid in the cradle of the house. . . . Life begins well, it begins enclosed, protected, all warm in the bosom of the house.

Then Zuboff adds her own commentary:

> Home is our school of intimacy, where we first learn to be human. Its corners and nooks conceal the sweetness of solitude; its rooms frame our experience of relationship. Its shelter, stability, and security work to concentrate our unique inner sense of self, an identity that imbues our day dreams and night dreams forever. Its hiding places—closets, chests, drawers, locks, and keys—satisfy our need for mystery and independence. Doors—locked, closed, half shut, wide open—trigger our sense of wonder, safety, possibility, and adventure.

2. Martin Buber, *Between Man & Man* (New York: Macmillan, 1947), 126.
3. Buber, 131, 133.
4. Micheal O'Siadhail, *The Five Quintets* (Waco, TX: Baylor University Press, 2018), 244.

5. Peter Berger, Brigitte Berger, and Hansfried Kellner, *The Homeless Mind: Modernization and Consciousness* (New York: Vintage Books, 1974). Much more programmatically, Jacques Ellul, *The Technological Society* (New York: Knopf, 1964), probes the impact of the displacing work of technology. Dennis M. Weiss, in *Design, Mediation, and the Posthuman* (Dennis M. Weiss, Amy D. Propen, and Colbey Emmerson Reid, eds. Lanham, Md: Lexington Books, 2016), has advanceds and critiquesd the discussion to which Buber and Berger are contributors.

6. Zuboff avers: "My house, my street, my neighborhood, my favorite café: each is redefined as a living tourist brochure, surveillance target, and strip mine, an object for universal inspection and commercial expropriation." *Age of Surveillance Capitalism,* 142.

7. Zuboff, 5.

8. Craig Fuller, "The Homeless Industrial Complex Problem," *HuffPost*, January 28, 2016, updated January 27, 2017, https://www.huffpost.com/entry/the-homeless -industrial-c_b_9092426.

9. See David Brooks, "The Case for Reparations," *New York Times*, March 8, 2019.

10. For a case in point, see the personal reportage of Kevin Roose, "How I Ditched My Phone and Unbroke My Brain," *New York Times*, February 23, 2019.

11. Zuboff, *Age of Surveillance Capitalism*, 520, 525.

12. In 1928, Sumner Welles (sometime undersecretary of state) issued an extended study of the predatory policies of the United States toward Central America and especially the Dominican Republic. He shrewdly titled his study "Naboth's Vineyard." By this title Welles suggested that the United States had played Ahab and Jezebel toward the vulnerable Naboth of the weak republic. This displacing role of Ahab and Jezebel toward the United States' southern neighbor may give us an extended pause as we face the plight of refugees from the southern border; the refugees are displaced as a legacy of the United States' long-term predatory policies there.

13. Patrick Phillips, *Blood at the Root: A Racial Cleansing in America* (New York: W. W. Norton, 2016), details the way in which African Americans were violently removed from Forsythe County, Georgia, in recent time. As they were forced to leave, whites occupied their property, paid the property taxes, and in a few years became the owners of the property by confiscation. This is a contemporary case of "moving boundaries"!

14. This is at the center of Wendell Berry's entire corpus of deeply moving writing. See, for example, *The Unsettling of America: Culture and Agriculture* (San Francisco: Sierra Club, 1977).

15. Saskia Sassen writes: "In the United States, the expansion of the high-income work force in conjunction with the emergence of new cultural forms has led to a process of high-income gentrification that rests, in the last analysis, on the availability of a vast supply of low-wage workers. High-income gentrification is labor intensive. . . . Directly or indirectly, high-income gentrification replaces much of this capital intensity with workers." *Cities in a World Economy*, 4th ed. (New York: Sage, 2012), 268.

16. Berry, *Unsettling of America*, 31; see Ellen F. Davis, *Scripture, Culture, and Agriculture: An Agrarian Reading of the Bible* (Cambridge: Cambridge University Press, 2009), 108.

17. Wuthnow provides a suggestive characterization of the distinctiveness of rural life. He especially champions its rich "associational life": "Rural communities are awash in such organizations. To be a respected member of the community means not only taking care of yourself and your family but also to pitch in to help in small ways to address the community's problems" (*The Left Behind*, 80). See David Brooks, "What Rural America Has to Teach Us," *New York Times*, March 22, 2019.

Conversely Zuboff writes of the city as the locus of displacement and dark data: "There is one place where all these elements come together and transform a shared public space built for human engagement into a petri dish for the reality business of surveillance capitalism. That place is the city" (*Age of Surveillance Capitalism*, 227). She further characterizes the city as "for-profit" by extraction, as a zone of "digital inequality," and its kiosks as "fountains of data."

18. Joseph Brackett Jr., "'Tis the Gift to Be Simple," *Hymnal 1982: According to the Use of the Episcopal Church* (New York: Church Hymnal Corp., 1985), 554.

19. See Wendell Berry, *The Gift of the Good Land: Further Essays Cultural and Agriculture* (San Francisco: North Point Press, 1981). Every place as the "right place" is a gift!

20. David Brooks, "An Agenda for Moderates," *New York Times*, February 26, 2019. See Wendell Berry, *It All Turns on Affection: The Jefferson Lecture and Other Essays* (Berkeley, CA: Counterpoint, 2012).

Conclusion

1. José Miranda, *Marx and the Bible: A Critique of the Philosophy of Oppression* (Maryknoll, NY: Orbis Books, 1974), 49.